Catalog of Homes

MILL-BUILT CLASSIC AMERICAN HOMES

Designs by Connor Homes

Architectural Integrity

The article "Master Class" by Bruce D. Snider appeared in its entirety in the July/August 2011 issue of Custom Home

WHY BUILD A HOUSE ON SITE if you can build it under controlled conditions with better tools in a shop? That line of thinking led Michael Connor, fresh out of college in 1969, to start a business erecting panelized houses. "I became a dealer for [a manufacturer in upstate New York]. I began selling houses and putting them up." Compared to traditional methods, panelization offered obvious advantages, he says. "The costs were better, the quality was better, the speed was there." The shortcomings he saw were not in the method but in the architecture to which it was applied. "Most [panelizers] pretty much ignored the aesthetic side," says Connor, who remembers thinking, "Why wouldn't you apply those same efficiencies to trim details?" Filling that blind spot would become the mission of Connor Homes, whose panelized custom houses combine advanced manufacturing techniques with painstakingly authentic traditional architecture.

"As far back as 1992 we had our catalog of houses - designed by my wife," Connor says. To replicate period details accurately, "we studied all kinds of plans, and actual houses." For their first Greek Revival house, the couple found an original they liked. "We knocked on the door and asked if we could stand up ladders and do some measurements." That deceptively simple approach - going back to the source - set Connor's work apart. Historical authenticity, he observes, "is about scale and proportion. And scale and proportion are free. You just have to know what they are and you can add incredible value - for nothing." Having started out as a general contractor working with a manufacturer's designs, Connor first shifted to designing and producing all of the houses he built, then to manufacturing house packages for other builders to assemble.

On a typical project, Connor Homes delivers a panelized shell and prefabricated exterior trim assemblies and interior millwork to a local contractor. "They pretty much run the show from there on," furnishing foundation, masonry, mechanical, electrical, drywall, paint and roofing, Connor explains. "Our total value is generally about one-third of the cost." Local contractors vary in skill level, he admits, "but we do all the sophisticated stuff, so it's pretty hard to mess up. We tell builders that if they need us, we'll come to the site. We'll drop everything. And it's an easy promise to make, because we've never had to do it. There's never been a problem we couldn't handle over the phone." From his base in Vermont, Connor does most of his business in the Northeast and Mid-Atlantic states, but he has delivered houses to sites as distant as British Columbia. "We're kind of in a niche by ourselves," Connor notes. While prefabrication and panelization are not unknown in the custom home industry, among those offering traditional designs, "nobody does as much stuff in the shop ahead of time as we do." But it is the company's high standard of architectural authenticity that truly sets it apart.

Traditional architecture remains overwhelmingly popular, Connor observes, but it is often "dumbed down" to reduce cost. The efficiency of shop fabrication, he says, permits a higher level of detail per dollar. With six designers on staff and standing relationships with several independent architects, Connor Homes has an impresive knack for making new houses that read like vintage pieces. That result, Connor says, is as important to the company as efficiency in production. "We want to leave a mark on the architectural landscape."

Photos on these pages
by Jim Westphalen

Photo by Jim Westphalen

1741 ROUTE 7 SOUTH | MIDDLEBURY, VERMONT | (802)382-9082
INFO@CONNORBUILDING.COM | WWW.CONNORBUILDING.COM

CONTENTS

DESIGNING AND BUILDING A CONNOR HOME

Connor Homes is a custom design and building company and, as a result, no two clients have exactly the same experience, but the following describes the general path that most of our clients take to design and build their Connor Home. See the chapter on "Design Services" or contact a Sales Associate to better understand the process.

phase one EXPLORATORY	Suggestions: make an appointment with a Connor Homes Sales Associate, see completed Connor homes in your area, search for and purchase land, set a budget, choose your favorite homes in our catalog, or complete a "Getting Started" Questionnaire (available from your Sales Associate).			*Timeline varies by client*
phase two SCHEMATIC DESIGN	Choose a Simple Classic and skip this phase.	Choose a Timeless Classic and make minor modifications.	Work with a Connor Homes Designer on a custom design.	*Timeline varies by path*
phase three DUE DILIGENCE	Use quotes from Connor Homes to request bids from local general contractors, or choose to work with the Connor Homes Field Crew. Acquire financing.			*1-3 months*
phase four COMMITMENT	Place a deposit. Continue Design Development. Choose a builder and sign a contract. Sign off on plans. Acquire permits. (All Connor Homes plans are designed to national and local code standards.) Construction drawings begin after sign-off.			*1 month*
phase five CONSTRUCTION I	In our Mill: Your framing and exterior trim packages will be built and stored safely until your site is ready, then shipped directly to you.		At your site: Your general contractor will tend to excavation, install utilities, and do other necessary site work.	*1 month*
phase six CONSTRUCTION II	At Connor Homes: Work with our Interior Designer to select trim, cabinetry, built-ins and other finishes. *An Interior Catalog is available for this phase.*		At your site: The shell is erected within a few days, followed by exterior trim, insulation, masonry, mechanicals, dry wall, etc.	*1-3 months*
phase seven FINISH CONSTRUCTION	In our Mill: Your interior finish package is built and stored safely until your home is ready.		At your site: Trim, flooring, cabinetry and built-ins are installed, and the house is painted.	*1-2 months*
phase eight ENJOY!	Move in, enjoy your new Connor home, and don't forget to send us photos of your completed home!			

9

FROM OUR CLIENTS

"I have spent the last week cleaning the house. Having touched every surface with a dust rag, I earned new appreciation for the detail and beauty of the house. I just can't thank you enough. The place is absolutely beautiful!!!!! And it is a true work of art. I would like to thank you for an enjoyable experience from Day One. Even though we knew very little about architecture, [the Design Team] both respected our opinions and wishes, and we had a lot of fun during the extremely creative process. The building and the detailing are phenomenal. I don't know exactly who is responsible for seeing to each and every thing, but I would like to send my thanks to each one of them."

Homeowner, Mallets Bay, Vermont

one

TIMELESS CLASSICS

THE EMMALINE GABRIELLE HOUSE

2,905 Square Feet

"*Walpole, New Hampshire is one of those perfect New England villages dotted with centuries- old houses. One home in particular has generated a lot of attention recently...'People tell me they think it's the most beautiful house on the street.'*"

"Home Maker"
by Suki Casanave
Attache, November 2005

Photos on this page by Jim Westphalen

12

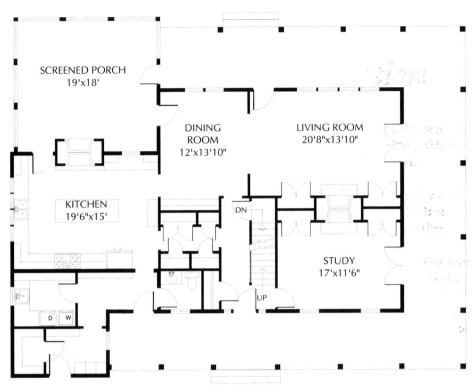

SCREENED PORCH
19'x18'

DINING
ROOM
12'x13'10"

LIVING ROOM
20'8"x13'10"

KITCHEN
19'6"x15'

DN

STUDY
17'x11'6"

UP

D W

FIRST FLOOR

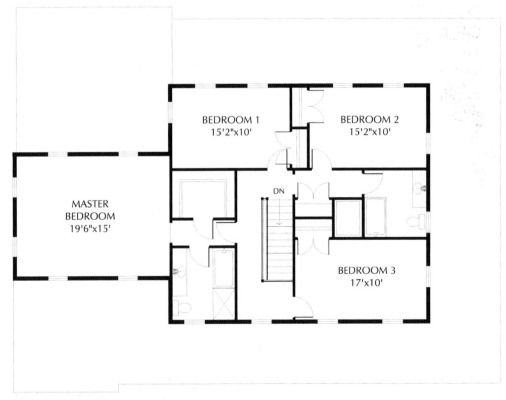

MASTER
BEDROOM
19'6"x15'

BEDROOM 1
15'2"x10'

BEDROOM 2
15'2"x10'

DN

BEDROOM 3
17'x10'

SECOND FLOOR

13

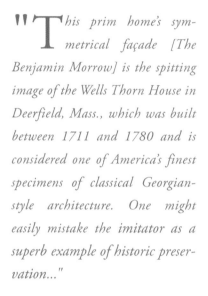

"This prim home's symmetrical façade [The Benjamin Morrow] is the spitting image of the Wells Thorn House in Deerfield, Mass., which was built between 1711 and 1780 and is considered one of America's finest specimens of classical Georgian-style architecture. One might easily mistake the imitator as a superb example of historic preservation..."

"Imagine That" by Jenny Sullivan
Builder Magazine
February 2011

Photos on these pages
by Jim Westphalen

THE BENJAMIN MORROW HOUSE

2,015 Square Feet

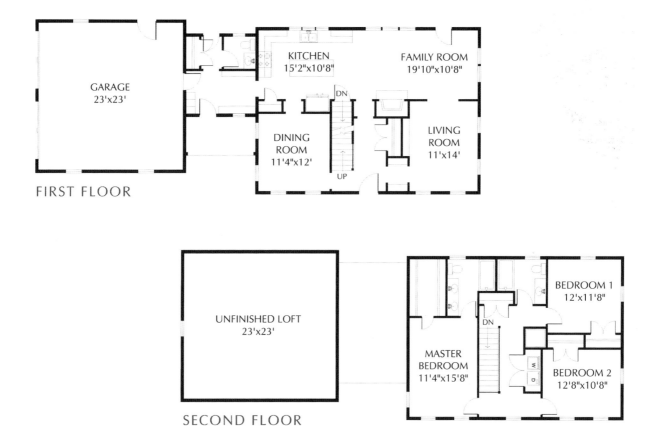

FIRST FLOOR

GARAGE
23'x23'

KITCHEN
15'2"x10'8"

FAMILY ROOM
19'10"x10'8"

DN

DINING
ROOM
11'4"x12'

UP

LIVING
ROOM
11'x14'

SECOND FLOOR

UNFINISHED LOFT
23'x23'

DN

BEDROOM 1
12'x11'8"

MASTER
BEDROOM
11'4"x15'8"

W
D

BEDROOM 2
12'8"x10'8"

Photo by Jim Westphalen

THE ELIZABETH BURGESS HOUSE

1,968 Square Feet

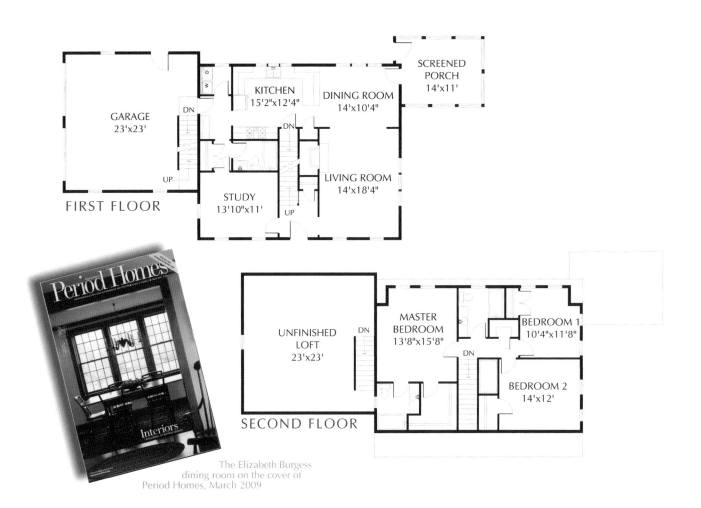

FIRST FLOOR

GARAGE
23'x23'

DN

UP

KITCHEN
15'2"x12'4"

DINING ROOM
14'x10'4"

SCREENED
PORCH
14'x11'

DN

STUDY
13'10"x11'

UP

LIVING ROOM
14'x18'4"

SECOND FLOOR

UNFINISHED
LOFT
23'x23'

DN

MASTER
BEDROOM
13'8"x15'8"

DN

BEDROOM 1
10'4"x11'8"

BEDROOM 2
14'x12'

The Elizabeth Burgess
dining room on the cover of
Period Homes, March 2009

THE ANNALINE SYRUS HOUSE

2,168 Square Feet

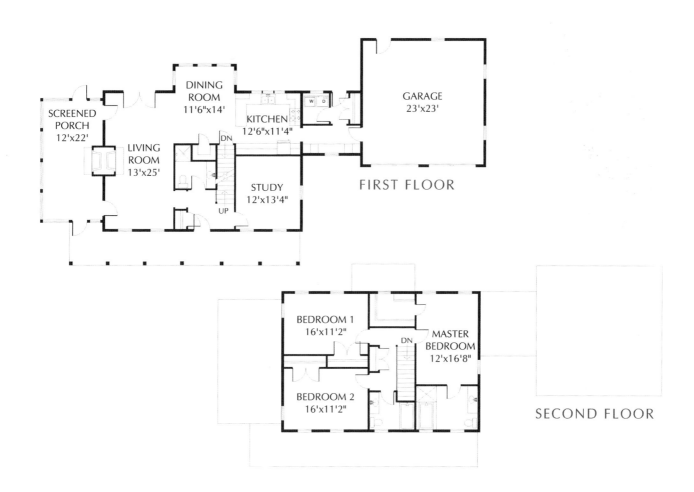

SCREENED PORCH 12'x22'

DINING ROOM 11'6"x14'

KITCHEN 12'6"x11'4"

W | D

GARAGE 23'x23'

LIVING ROOM 13'x25'

DN

UP

STUDY 12'x13'4"

FIRST FLOOR

BEDROOM 1 16'x11'2"

DN

MASTER BEDROOM 12'x16'8"

BEDROOM 2 16'x11'2"

SECOND FLOOR

THE HANNAH GRADY HOUSE

1,733 Square Feet

DINING ROOM
11'x12'

LIVING ROOM
22'x12'

DN

KITCHEN
11'x14'8"

UP

STUDY
11'x12'

FIRST FLOOR

MASTER BEDOOM
11'x13'8"

DN

BEDROOM 1
13'x10'6"

D W

BEDROOM 2
13'x9'

SECOND FLOOR

THE ALEXANDER YOUNGMAN HOUSE

1,942 Square Feet

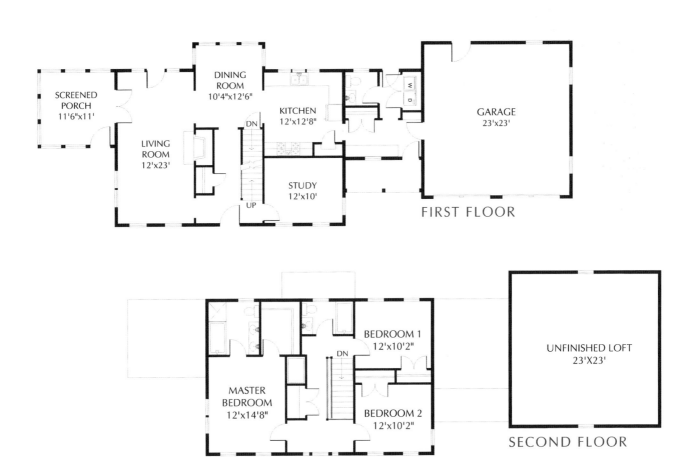

SCREENED
PORCH
11'6"x11'

DINING
ROOM
10'4"x12'6"

KITCHEN
12'x12'8"

LIVING
ROOM
12'x23'

DN

STUDY
12'x10'

UP

GARAGE
23'x23'

FIRST FLOOR

MASTER
BEDROOM
12'x14'8"

BEDROOM 1
12'x10'2"

DN

BEDROOM 2
12'x10'2"

UNFINISHED LOFT
23'X23'

SECOND FLOOR

HISTORY AND CHARACTER

The Greek Revival style was in favor from the 1830s to the 1870s. Columns, porticos and pediments were used to closely mimic the Greek temples for which the period is named. Emphasis remained on the front entry and entries were often recessed and flanked by sidelites rather than a fanlite or transom. It was common to see the gable end, or pediment, facing the street with the entry placed to one side.

The Hesther Burr House is an example of this style. The framing and exterior trim of this southern Virginia home were installed with a 10-man crew in nine days, earning the house the nickname "The 9-Day Greek Revival". The homeowners completed the rest of the home themselves, an undertaking made possible with a Connor Homes mill-built package.

Kitchen in the Dorothea Harwell House

Photo by Jim Westphalen

THE HESTHER BURR HOUSE

3,134 Square Feet

FIRST FLOOR

GARAGE
23'x31'

KITCHEN
15'6"x16'4"

DINING ROOM
13'2"x13'8"

STUDY
17'6"x13'8"

SCREENED PORCH
17'x9'8"

BEDROOM
14'8"x16'8"

LIVING ROOM
17'6"x21'

DN

UP

SECOND FLOOR

BEDROOM 1
12'8"x13'4"

BEDROOM 2
12'8"x13'4"

DN

MASTER BEDROOM
17'4"x13'

THE ABIGAIL BEARCE HOUSE

1,774 Square Feet

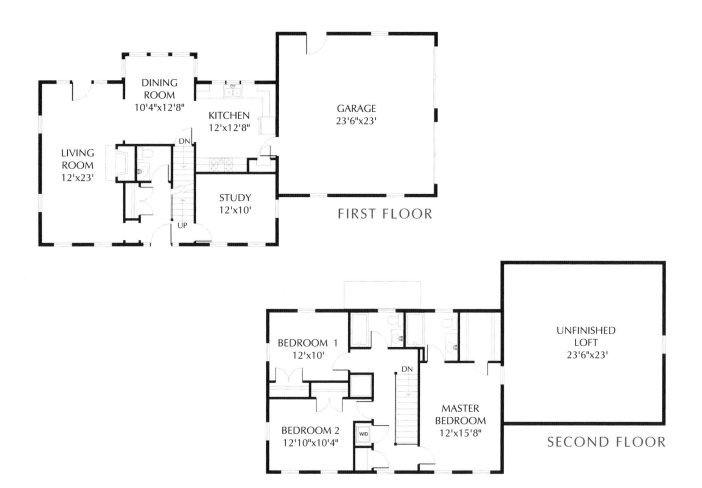

DINING
ROOM
10'4"x12'8"

KITCHEN
12'x12'8"

GARAGE
23'6"x23'

DN

LIVING
ROOM
12'x23'

STUDY
12'x10'

UP

FIRST FLOOR

BEDROOM 1
12'x10'

UNFINISHED
LOFT
23'6"x23'

DN

BEDROOM 2
12'10"x10'4"

W/D

MASTER
BEDROOM
12'x15'8"

SECOND FLOOR

THE McCLELLAN FARMHOUSE

2,322 Square Feet

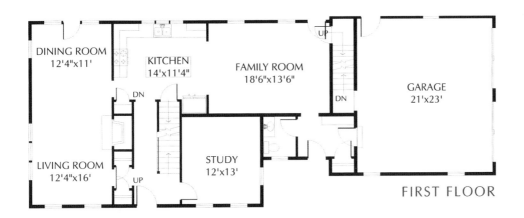

DINING ROOM
12'4"x11'

KITCHEN
14'x11'4"

FAMILY ROOM
18'6"x13'6"

GARAGE
21'x23'

DN

DN

UP

LIVING ROOM
12'4"x16'

UP

STUDY
12'x13'

FIRST FLOOR

BEDROOM 1
12'4"x11'4"

W D

DN

UNFINISHED
LOFT
25'x23'

DN

MASTER
BEDROOM
12'x18'10"

BEDROOM 2
12'4"x12'2"

SECOND FLOOR

THE LUELLA GREGORY HOUSE

2,654 Square Feet

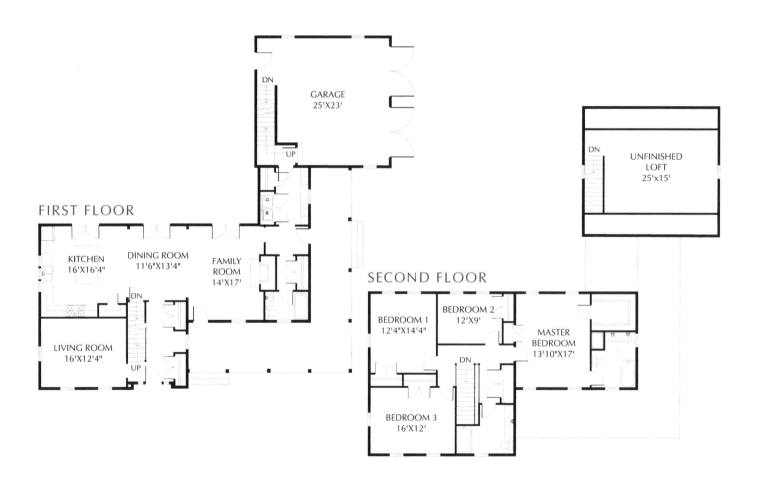

FIRST FLOOR

DN

GARAGE
25'X23'

UP

W D

KITCHEN
16'X16'4"

DINING ROOM
11'6"X13'4"

FAMILY
ROOM
14'X17'

DN

LIVING ROOM
16'X12'4"

UP

SECOND FLOOR

BEDROOM 1
12'4"X14'4"

BEDROOM 2
12'X9'

MASTER
BEDROOM
13'10"X17'

DN

BEDROOM 3
16'X12'

DN

UNFINISHED
LOFT
25'x15'

The Luella Gregory has been a popular home design among our clients, who have each made minor modifications to the floorplan to make it their own. Below, Luella Gregorys from Vermont and upstate New York, where this Greek Revival style is traditionally prevalent.

FROM OUR CLIENTS

"On a regular basis we get compliments on the house from friends, acquaintances and even strangers. When people ask where I live, I describe the location, and they usually say, "Oh I love that house". Someone was running by recently and yelled out, "Best new construction in the area". Our favorite is when people say "Your house is so pretty. It looks like it's always been here" - the ultimate compliment and we hear it several times a month.

The most important thing is that we just love this house. It's cozy for the two of us and roomy enough when our kids or friends visit. It's just beautiful. Every day I pinch myself. It's really mine! Thanks again."

Homeowner, Woodstock, Vermont

THE AMY FOSCOTT HOUSE

1,760 Square Feet

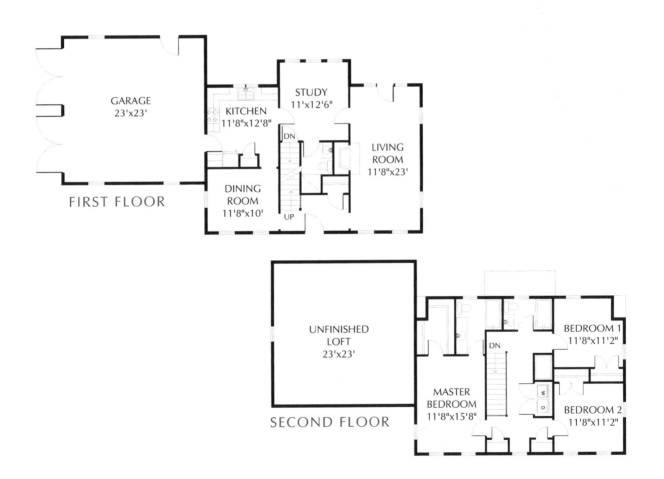

FIRST FLOOR

- GARAGE 23'x23'
- KITCHEN 11'8"x12'8"
- STUDY 11'x12'6"
- LIVING ROOM 11'8"x23'
- DINING ROOM 11'8"x10'
- DN
- UP

SECOND FLOOR

- UNFINISHED LOFT 23'x23'
- MASTER BEDROOM 11'8"x15'8"
- BEDROOM 1 11'8"x11'2"
- BEDROOM 2 11'8"x11'2"
- DN
- W
- D

THE VIRGINIA GILL HOUSE

2,225 Square Feet

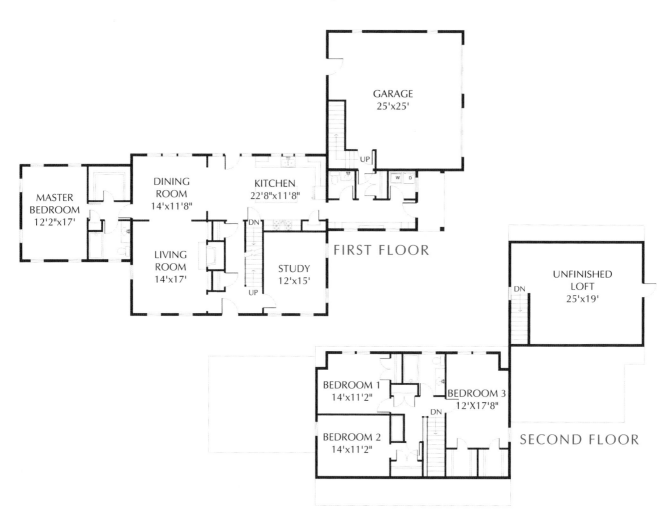

GARAGE
25'x25'

MASTER
BEDROOM
12'2"x17'

DINING
ROOM
14'x11'8"

KITCHEN
22'8"x11'8"

UP

W   D

LIVING
ROOM
14'x17'

DN

STUDY
12'x15'

UP

FIRST FLOOR

UNFINISHED
LOFT
25'x19'

DN

BEDROOM 1
14'x11'2"

BEDROOM 3
12'X17'8"

DN

BEDROOM 2
14'x11'2"

SECOND FLOOR

THE JOSEPH ABERCROMBIE HOUSE

2,622 Square Feet

FIRST FLOOR

SECOND FLOOR

THE CHARLOTTE PRINDLE HOUSE

2,586 Square Feet

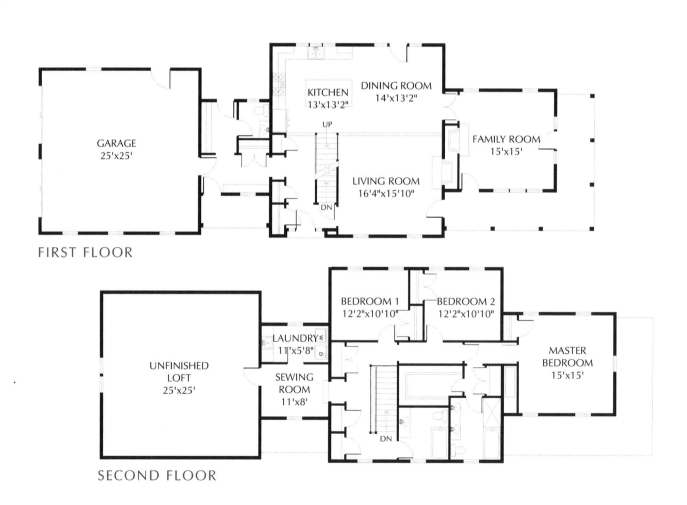

FIRST FLOOR

GARAGE
25'x25'

KITCHEN
13'x13'2"

DINING ROOM
14'x13'2"

UP

FAMILY ROOM
15'x15'

LIVING ROOM
16'4"x15'10"

DN

SECOND FLOOR

UNFINISHED
LOFT
25'x25'

LAUNDRY
11'x5'8"

SEWING
ROOM
11'x8'

BEDROOM 1
12'2"x10'10"

BEDROOM 2
12'2"x10'10"

MASTER
BEDROOM
15'x15'

DN

OUR CLIENTS OFTEN MAKE *minor modifications to the homes in the Timeless Classics Collection, so throughout the catalog, you may notice discrepancies between the floor plan shown and photos of the house, like the location of the fireplace in this Charlotte Prindle.*

THE MERCY WELDON HOUSE

2,792 Square Feet

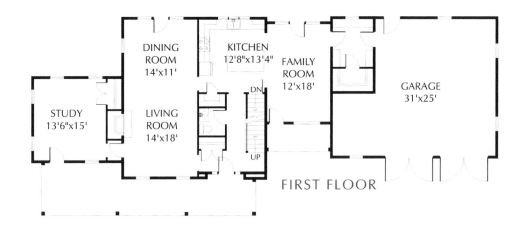

STUDY
13'6"x15'

DINING
ROOM
14'x11'

KITCHEN
12'8"x13'4"

LIVING
ROOM
14'x18'

FAMILY
ROOM
12'x18'

DN

UP

GARAGE
31'x25'

FIRST FLOOR

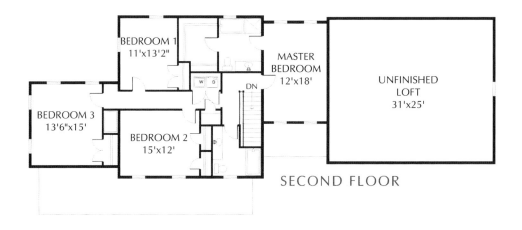

BEDROOM 1
11'x13'2"

BEDROOM 3
13'6"x15'

BEDROOM 2
15'x12'

W   D

MASTER
BEDROOM
12'x18'

DN

UNFINISHED
LOFT
31'x25'

SECOND FLOOR

NEARLY 500 CONNOR HOMES *grace the landscape of the northeast and are often mistaken for historic homes. Here are just a few of our favorite variations: an Eli Thatcher in Massachusetts; a Hannah Grady in a Vermont village; a Martha Kimball in Massachusetts; a Jeremiah Lee in Connecticut; an Augustine Parker in Vermont; and the rear of an Emmaline Gabrielle with a sunroom and attached barn in New York.*

Photo by Jim Westphalen

THE SARAH TAYLOR HOUSE

2,680 Square Feet

"It's hard to believe the charming Sarah Taylor House was built this year...this production house is a perfect example of a growing trend in the new old house market."

"House in a Box" by Russell Versaci
New Old House, Winter 2007

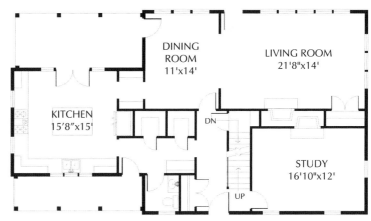

DINING ROOM
11'x14'

LIVING ROOM
21'8"x14'

KITCHEN
15'8"x15'

DN

STUDY
16'10"x12'

UP

FIRST FLOOR

SECOND FLOOR

BEDROOM 1
15'2"x10'4"

BEDROOM 2
15'2"x10'4"

W   D

DN

MASTER BEDROOM
15'x15'2"

BEDROOM 3
14'6"x11'10"

Any of the homes in our catalog can be easily "mirrored" or modified to include a barn and mudroom, like these Sarah Taylors built in Massachusetts, New York and Vermont.

35

THE MARTHA KIMBALL HOUSE

2,443 Square Feet

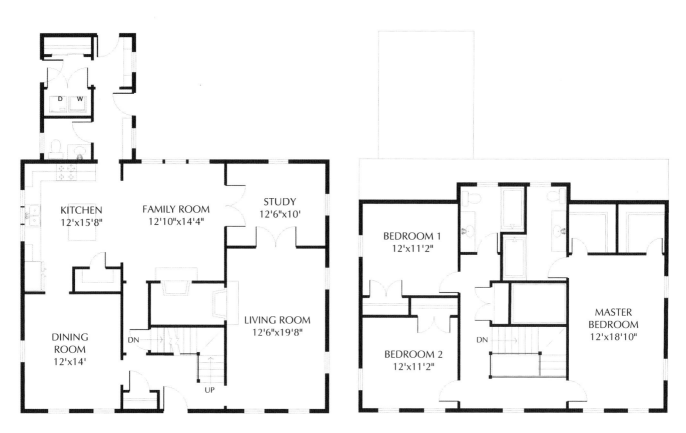

KITCHEN
12'x15'8"

FAMILY ROOM
12'10"x14'4"

STUDY
12'6"x10'

DINING
ROOM
12'x14'

DN

LIVING ROOM
12'6"x19'8"

UP

BEDROOM 1
12'x11'2"

MASTER
BEDROOM
12'x18'10"

DN

BEDROOM 2
12'x11'2"

FIRST FLOOR

SECOND FLOOR

HISTORY AND CHARACTER

This Salt Box reproduction home, built in 1999, has the distinctive "saltbox" roof that has its roots in the 14th century English "catslide" roofs, which were extensions of existing houses. American "saltbox" roofs were usually, but not always, a result of adding a one-story shed to the back of the house and then extending the roof down to shelter the new addition. Some early saltbox houses were built with the "catslide" as part of the original design as we do today. One possible clue to the latter version is the different roof pitches front and back as in our Martha Kimball House.

Photo by Jean Westphalen

STUNNING INTERIOR MILLWORK
is just one of the features that sets Connor
Homes apart from other home manufacturers
and builders.

Photos on these pages by Jim Westphalen

THE OLIVER HAINES HOUSE

3,144 Square Feet

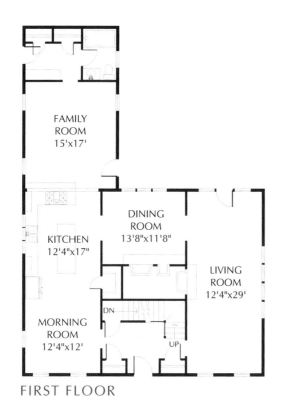

FAMILY
ROOM
15'x17'

KITCHEN
12'4"x17"

DINING
ROOM
13'8"x11'8"

LIVING
ROOM
12'4"x29'

DN

MORNING
ROOM
12'4"x12'

UP

FIRST FLOOR

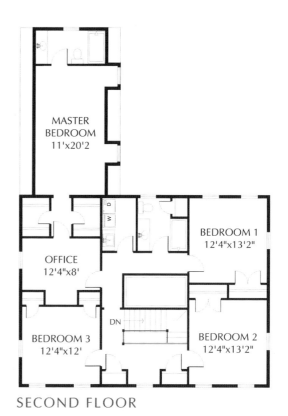

MASTER
BEDROOM
11'x20'2

OFFICE
12'4"x8'

BEDROOM 1
12'4"x13'2"

DN

BEDROOM 3
12'4"x12'

BEDROOM 2
12'4"x13'2"

SECOND FLOOR

ROOMS IN THE OLIVER HAINES and several custom Connor homes: mill-built architecture combines talented designers with highly skilled craftsmen to produce an array of impeccable finishes, trims, cabinets and built-ins.

THE CAROLINE FARR HOUSE

2,450 Square Feet

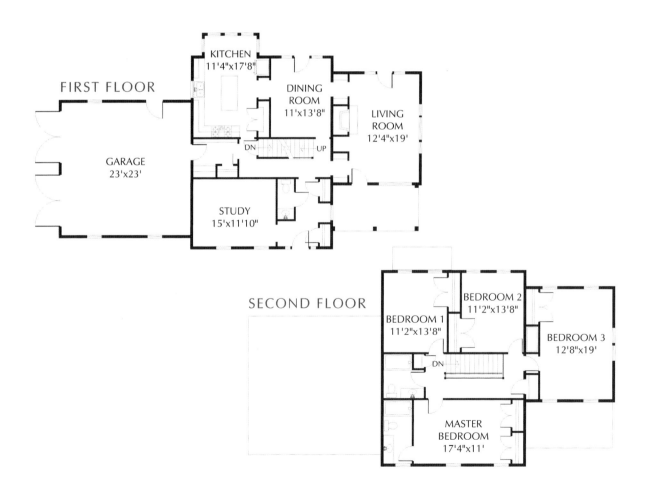

FIRST FLOOR

KITCHEN
11'4"x17'8"

DINING
ROOM
11'x13'8"

LIVING
ROOM
12'4"x19'

DN   UP

GARAGE
23'x23'

STUDY
15'x11'10"

SECOND FLOOR

BEDROOM 1
11'2"x13'8"

BEDROOM 2
11'2"x13'8"

BEDROOM 3
12'8"x19'

DN

MASTER
BEDROOM
17'4"x11'

THE JANE BLACKABY HOUSE

1,927 Square Feet

KITCHEN
11'4"x14'8"

FAMILY ROOM
21'8"x12'

DN

DINING ROOM
11'x14'

LIVING ROOM
13'x16'8"

UP

FIRST FLOOR

BEDROOM 2
11'x10'8"

DN

MASTER
BEDROOM
11'x15'

BEDROOM 1
15'x10'

SECOND FLOOR

FROM OUR CLIENTS

"Let me start by saying thank you for helping us build the house of our dreams. As I sit here thinking back over what a whirlwind it has been for first time homebuilders to have achieved such a rewarding end, I am glad that we chose your company for our new home. With such great technical support our builder said he would build another Connor home in a heartbeat. I think our home may be the most envied in the neighborhood. We have received so many compliments from family and friends as to the aesthetics of the house, and also to the design and quality of building materials used in construction. Our naysayer friends that warned of purchasing a home first, from out of state and second, with prebuilt construction were quite impressed."

Homeowner, Augusta, Ohio

Photo by Jim Westphalen

THE ELI THATCHER HOUSE

2,128 Square Feet

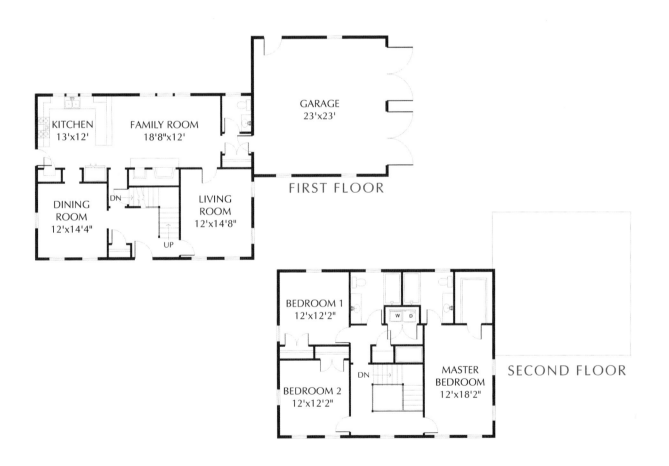

KITCHEN
13'x12'

FAMILY ROOM
18'8"x12'

GARAGE
23'x23'

DINING ROOM
12'x14'4"

DN

LIVING ROOM
12'x14'8"

UP

FIRST FLOOR

BEDROOM 1
12'x12'2"

W D

BEDROOM 2
12'x12'2"

DN

MASTER BEDROOM
12'x18'2"

SECOND FLOOR

THE LAVINIA WOOLSEY HOUSE

1,968 Square Feet

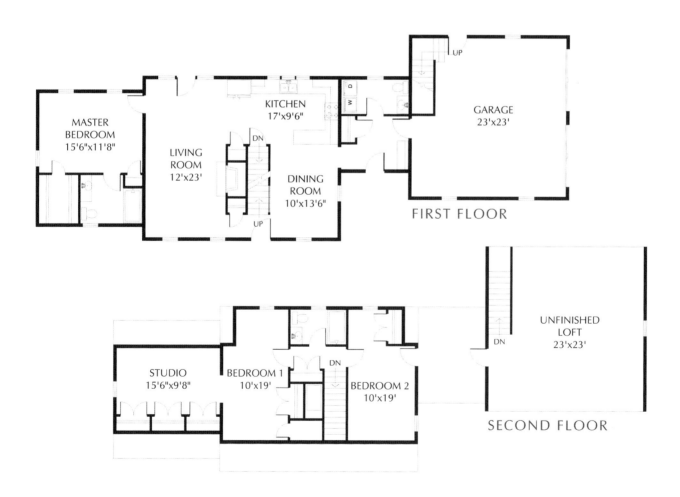

MASTER BEDROOM
15'6"x11'8"

LIVING ROOM
12'x23'

KITCHEN
17'x9'6"

DN

DINING ROOM
10'x13'6"

UP

GARAGE
23'x23'

UP

FIRST FLOOR

STUDIO
15'6"x9'8"

BEDROOM 1
10'x19'

DN

BEDROOM 2
10'x19'

UNFINISHED LOFT
23'x23'

DN

SECOND FLOOR

THE AUGUSTINE PARKER HOUSE

2,540 Square Feet

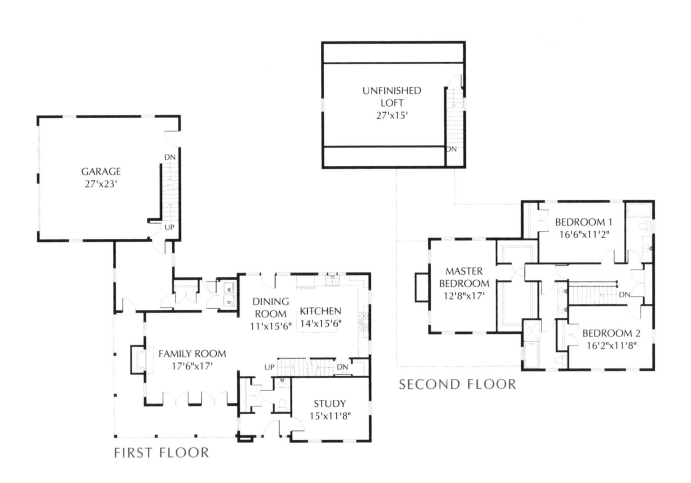

UNFINISHED LOFT
27'x15'

GARAGE
27'x23'

DN

UP

DINING ROOM
11'x15'6"

KITCHEN
14'x15'6"

FAMILY ROOM
17'6"x17'

UP   DN

STUDY
15'x11'8"

FIRST FLOOR

MASTER BEDROOM
12'8"x17'

BEDROOM 1
16'6"x11'2"

DN

BEDROOM 2
16'2"x11'8"

SECOND FLOOR

THE ELEANOR MOWBRAY HOUSE

3,060 Square Feet

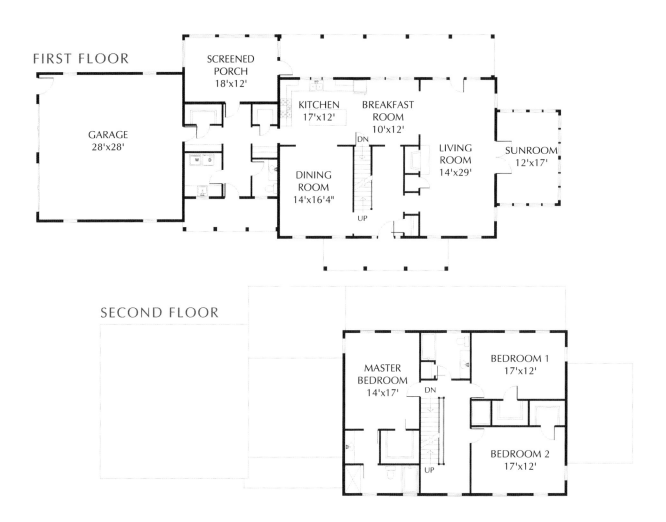

FIRST FLOOR

SCREENED
PORCH
18'x12'

KITCHEN
17'x12'

BREAKFAST
ROOM
10'x12'

GARAGE
28'x28'

DN

LIVING
ROOM
14'x29'

SUNROOM
12'x17'

W D

DINING
ROOM
14'x16'4"

UP

SECOND FLOOR

MASTER
BEDROOM
14'x17'

BEDROOM 1
17'x12'

DN

BEDROOM 2
17'x12'

UP

THE ELEANOR MOWBRAY HOUSE was built in our mills in Vermont and shipped to British Columbia. The incomparable workmanship of a Connor Home coupled with an innovative and efficient production process makes our homes a desirable and viable option across the globe. Our team will help find the most economical shipping method for you.

THE ANN HADAWAY HOUSE

1,672 Square Feet

LIVING ROOM
20'8"x12'

KITCHEN
10'x10'

MASTER BEDROOM
13'6"x12'8"

DN

DINING ROOM
10'x12'4"`

UP

FIRST FLOOR

BEDROOM 1
10'x14'

DN

BEDROOM 2
10'x14'

W

D

SECOND FLOOR

THE EMILY BLACK HOUSE

2,822 Square Feet

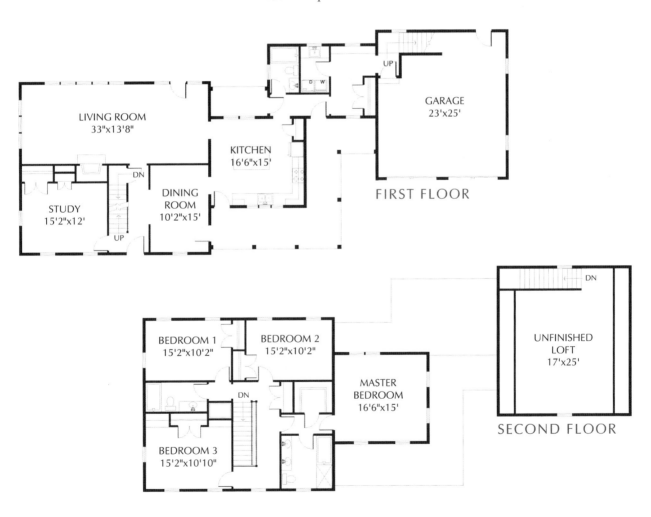

FIRST FLOOR

LIVING ROOM
33"x13'8"

STUDY
15'2"x12'

DINING
ROOM
10'2"x15'

KITCHEN
16'6"x15'

DN

UP

UP

D   W

GARAGE
23'x25'

SECOND FLOOR

BEDROOM 1
15'2"x10'2"

BEDROOM 2
15'2"x10'2"

BEDROOM 3
15'2"x10'10"

MASTER
BEDROOM
16'6"x15'

DN

UNFINISHED
LOFT
17'x25'

DN

THE NATHANIEL FOWLER HOUSE

3,930 Square Feet

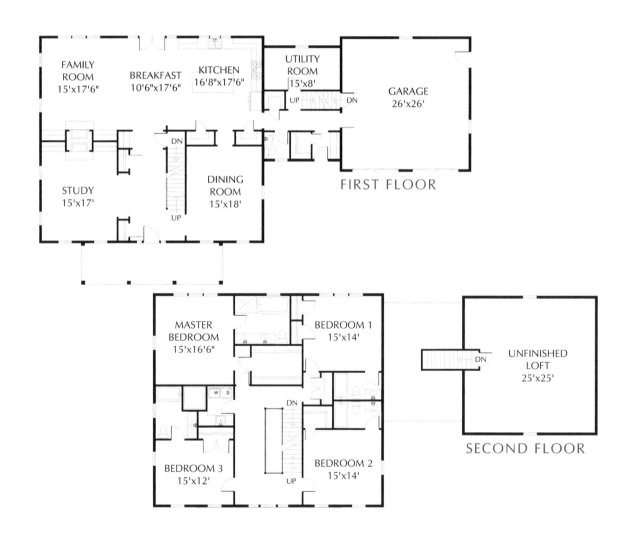

FIRST FLOOR

FAMILY ROOM 15'x17'6"
BREAKFAST 10'6"x17'6"
KITCHEN 16'8"x17'6"
UTILITY ROOM 15'x8'
GARAGE 26'x26'
UP DN
DN
STUDY 15'x17'
DINING ROOM 15'x18'
UP

SECOND FLOOR

MASTER BEDROOM 15'x16'6"
BEDROOM 1 15'x14'
UNFINISHED LOFT 25'x25'
DN
W D
DN
BEDROOM 3 15'x12'
BEDROOM 2 15'x14'
UP

HISTORY AND CHARACTER

The handsome Nathaniel Fowler House, and the detail of the Walter Edgecomb shown at left, feature a wide front porch, Palladian window and heavy Georgian era trim elements. The larger elements under the roofline are called modillions and the smaller elements below are called dentils. Note the fluted corner pilasters. Similar detailing can be found on the Dorothea Harwell and Benjamin Morrow Houses.

Interior detailing carries the outside mouldings in, and the use of arched doorways would have been common in the Georgian era.

THE KATE BANNEKER HOUSE

3,575 Square Feet

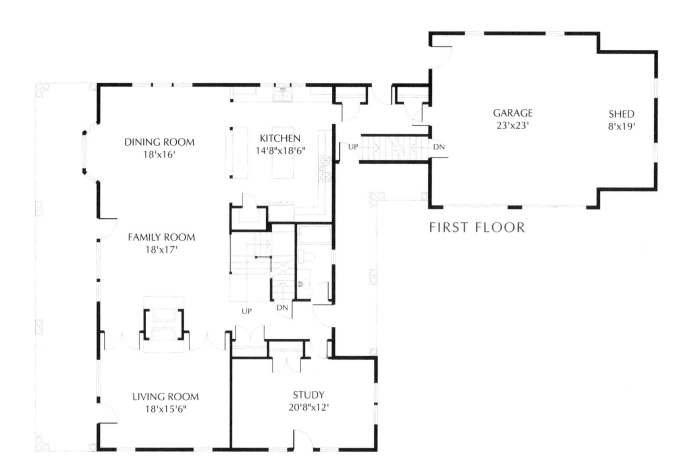

DINING ROOM
18'x16'

KITCHEN
14'8"x18'6"

UP   DN

GARAGE
23'x23'

SHED
8'x19'

FAMILY ROOM
18'x17'

FIRST FLOOR

UP   DN

LIVING ROOM
18'x15'6"

STUDY
20'8"x12'

MASTER
BEDROOM
18'x16'

LAUNDRY
13'x5'6"

W D

DN

UNFINISHED
LOFT
23'x19'

SECOND FLOOR

OPEN TO
BELOW

DN

BEDROOM 1
11'4"x13'

BEDROOM 2
12'8"x12'

BEDROOM 3
14'4"x12'

Details from several of our
shingle style homes

THE REBECCA LELAND HOUSE

3,282 Square Feet

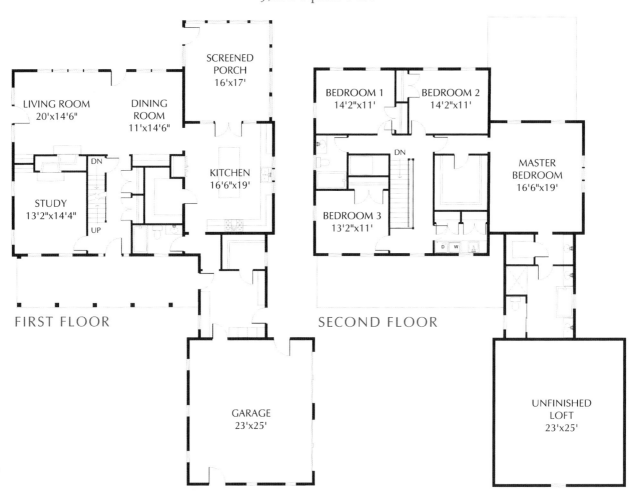

SCREENED
PORCH
16'x17'

LIVING ROOM
20'x14'6"

DINING
ROOM
11'x14'6"

STUDY
13'2"x14'4"

KITCHEN
16'6"x19'

DN

UP

FIRST FLOOR

BEDROOM 1
14'2"x11'

BEDROOM 2
14'2"x11'

DN

MASTER
BEDROOM
16'6"x19'

BEDROOM 3
13'2"x11'

D W

SECOND FLOOR

GARAGE
23'x25'

UNFINISHED
LOFT
23'x25'

THE REBECCA LELAND House was honored with LEED certification and was one of the subjects of the book "Pre-Fabulous + Sustainable" by Sherri Koones. Note the solar panes on the rear roof, and the reclaimed flooring and lighting fixtures used throughout the house. Whether seeking certification, or just sustainable living, a Connor home built of durable, green materials in a waste-limiting manufacturing process can accomplish both. Below, photos in "Pre-Fabulous + Sustainable" of the Rebecca Leland Farmhouse and the Connor Homes mill shop.

Photos on these pages by Jim Westphalen

THE PRISCILLA ELDREDGE HOUSE

2,664 Square Feet

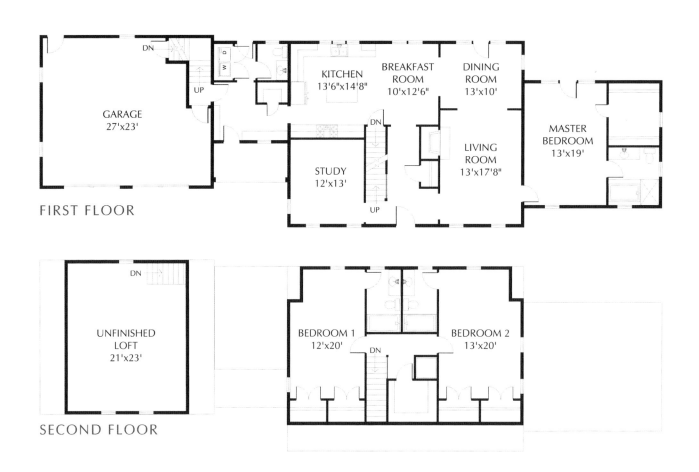

FIRST FLOOR

GARAGE
27'x23'

DN
UP
W
D

KITCHEN
13'6"x14'8"

BREAKFAST
ROOM
10'x12'6"

DINING
ROOM
13'x10'

MASTER
BEDROOM
13'x19'

DN

STUDY
12'x13'

UP

LIVING
ROOM
13'x17'8"

SECOND FLOOR

DN

UNFINISHED
LOFT
21'x23'

BEDROOM 1
12'x20'

BEDROOM 2
13'x20'

DN

THE LYDIA SHEPPEY HOUSE

2,408 Square Feet

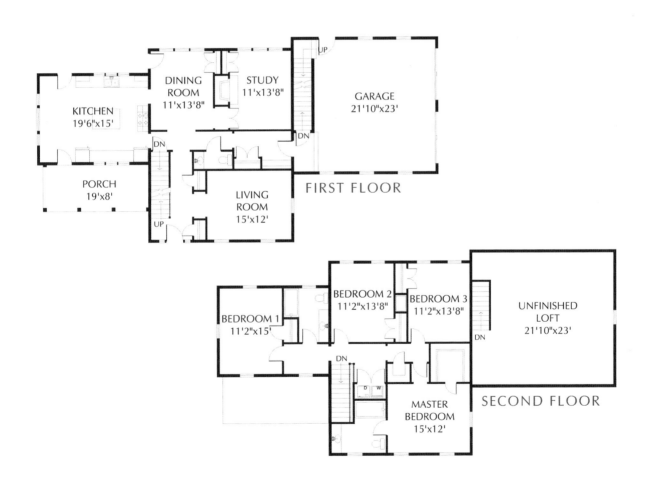

FROM OUR CLIENTS

"I knew as soon as I opened the door that this house would pass, look at the way these windows are framed, now that's the way you are supposed to frame windows." I asked if he would like to look at the second floor or in the crawl space. "No, this is the best constructed house I have seen for years, I don't have to see any more."

Comments from a homeowner's
70-year-old house inspector
Green Bay, Virginia

"The Energy Star test-out of your house went very well. It received the highest score yet for any ES house I have done."

Statement to a homeowner from an
Energy Star tester
Chatham, New York

"This morning I went for a run and stopped in front of the house and a woman who was driving by stopped and asked me if it was mine. She then told me that she thought "it was the nicest house in all of Southampton". I have had dozens of people say something to the same effect over the last month or so. Not too shabby praise."

A Connor homeowner with happy
neighbors
Southampton, New York

Photo by: Jim Westphalen

THE TABITHA WELLS HOUSE

2,424 Square Feet

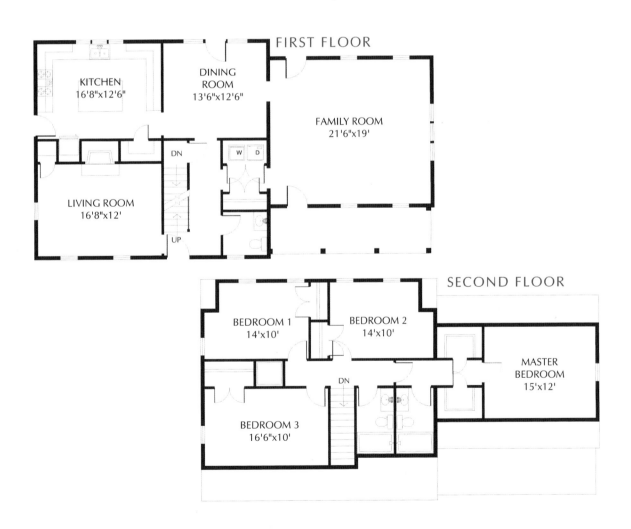

FIRST FLOOR

KITCHEN
16'8"x12'6"

DINING
ROOM
13'6"x12'6"

FAMILY ROOM
21'6"x19'

DN

W D

LIVING ROOM
16'8"x12'

UP

SECOND FLOOR

BEDROOM 1
14'x10'

BEDROOM 2
14'x10'

MASTER
BEDROOM
15'x12'

DN

BEDROOM 3
16'6"x10'

THE EDWARD SISSELL HOUSE

2,306 Square Feet

GARAGE
23'x23'

FIRST FLOOR

KITCHEN
15'2"x10'4"

DINING ROOM
14'x10'4"

MASTER
BEDROOM
12'x17'

STUDY
13'10"x11'

LIVING ROOM
14'16'4"

SCREENED
PORCH
8'6"x14'6"

DN

UP

SECOND FLOOR

BEDROOM 1
13'10"x17'8"

BEDROOM 2
10'2"x11'6"

BEDROOM 3
13'8"x10'6"

DN

Photos on this page
by Jim Westphalen

THE STEWART HAMIL LAKE COTTAGE

1,908 Square Feet

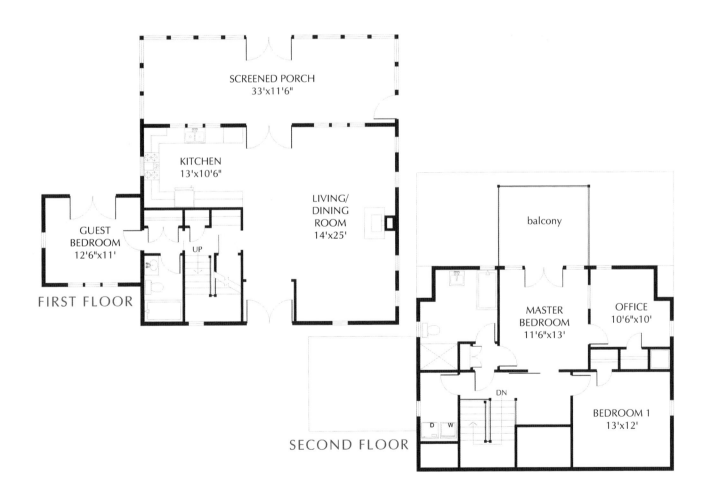

SCREENED PORCH
33'x11'6"

KITCHEN
13'x10'6"

LIVING/
DINING
ROOM
14'x25'

GUEST
BEDROOM
12'6"x11'

UP

FIRST FLOOR

balcony

MASTER
BEDROOM
11'6"x13'

OFFICE
10'6"x10'

DN

BEDROOM 1
13'x12'

D W

SECOND FLOOR

THE DOROTHEA HARWELL HOUSE

3,856 Square Feet

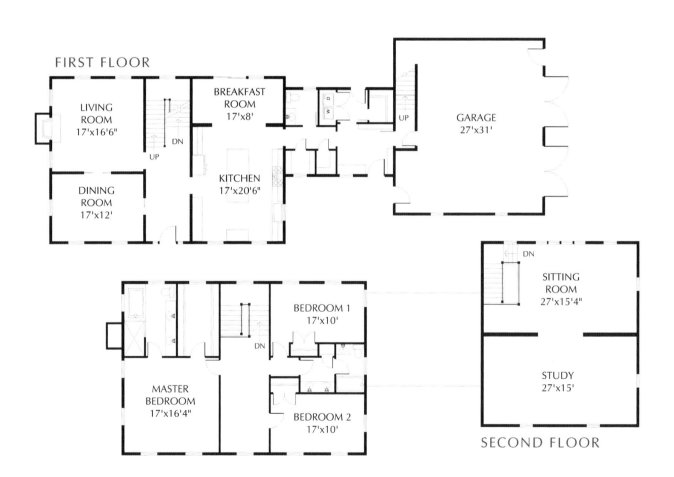

FIRST FLOOR

LIVING ROOM
17'x16'6"

DINING ROOM
17'x12'

BREAKFAST ROOM
17'x8'

KITCHEN
17'x20'6"

DN

UP

UP

W D

GARAGE
27'x31'

MASTER BEDROOM
17'x16'4"

BEDROOM 1
17'x10'

DN

BEDROOM 2
17'x10'

DN

SITTING ROOM
27'x15'4"

STUDY
27'x15'

SECOND FLOOR

The Dorothea Harwell was featured in the July/August 2011 issue of Custom Home, along with several other Connor homes.

65

Photo by Jim Westphalen

THE AZARIAH CANFIELD HOUSE

1,980 Square Feet

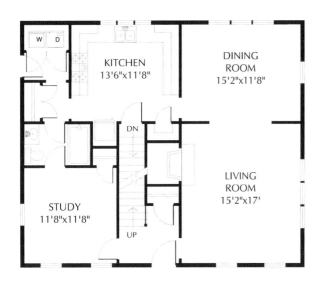

W D

KITCHEN
13'6"x11'8"

DINING
ROOM
15'2"x11'8"

DN

LIVING
ROOM
15'2"x17'

STUDY
11'8"x11'8"

UP

FIRST FLOOR

SECOND FLOOR

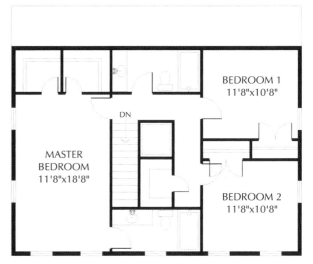

BEDROOM 1
11'8"x10'8"

DN

MASTER
BEDROOM
11'8"x18'8"

BEDROOM 2
11'8"x10'8"

THE SUSANNAH KINNICUTT HOUSE

USING THE AZARIAH CANFIELD FLOOR PLAN as a starting point, our talented architects transformed the primitive saltbox into a coastal two-story, the Susannah Kinnicutt.

If you see a floorplan that you like in these pages, but need a different style of home, or see a vernacular or type that you love, but the floor plan doesn't suit your needs, talk to our Sales Associates about modifying one of our homes. You can read more about the design process on page 108.

The porch on the Rebecca Leland House, with a standing seam metal roof

HISTORY AND CHARACTER

Although many people don't think of this story and a half house as Greek Revival, its wide, simple frieze, supported by heavy pilaster corners, and Greek order entry are all important elements of the Greek revival style. The style reached its heyday just prior to the Civil War, but continued to evolve in later styles. This particular version of Greek revival is quite commonly found throughout New England and upstate New York, and followed the expansion of the nation westward, so that many examples can be found in Western Pennsylvania, Ohio and beyond. These houses, although made of wood, still reflected the structural integrity of stone Greek temples.

Westphalen

THE JEREMIAH LEE HOUSE

2,370 Square Feet

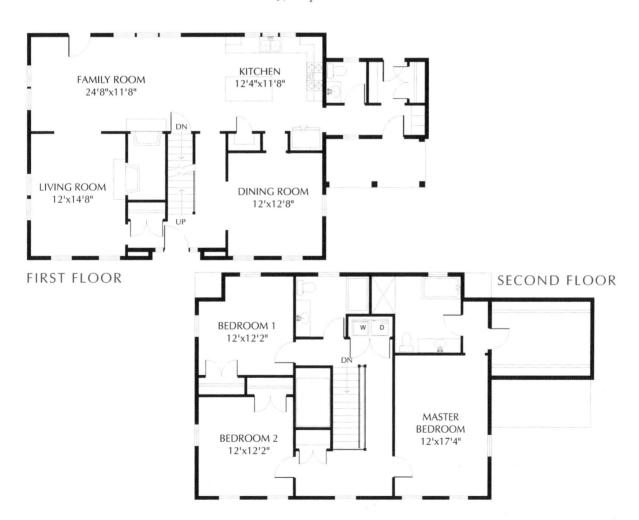

FAMILY ROOM
24'8"x11'8"

KITCHEN
12'4"x11'8"

DN

LIVING ROOM
12'x14'8"

DINING ROOM
12'x12'8"

UP

FIRST FLOOR

SECOND FLOOR

BEDROOM 1
12'x12'2"

W   D

DN

MASTER
BEDROOM
12'x17'4"

BEDROOM 2
12'x12'2"

THE BRIAN GRANT BRADY HOUSE

2,840 Square Feet

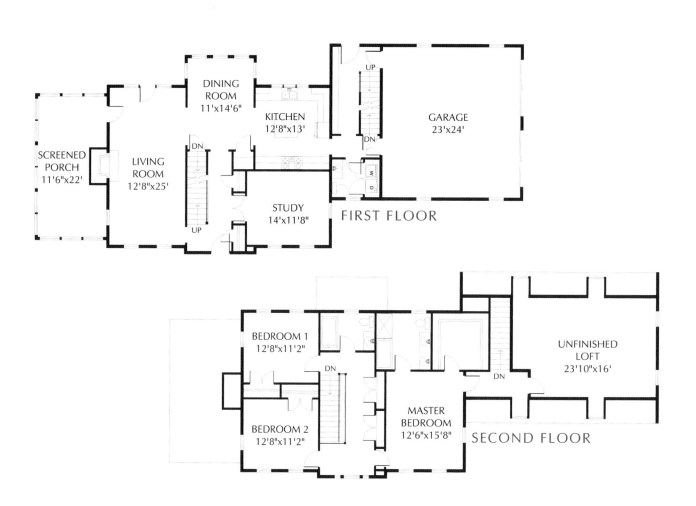

FIRST FLOOR

SCREENED PORCH 11'6"x22'

LIVING ROOM 12'8"x25'

DINING ROOM 11'x14'6"

KITCHEN 12'8"x13'

STUDY 14'x11'8"

GARAGE 23'x24'

UP

DN

DN

UP

W

D

SECOND FLOOR

BEDROOM 1 12'8"x11'2"

BEDROOM 2 12'8"x11'2"

MASTER BEDROOM 12'6"x15'8"

UNFINISHED LOFT 23'10"x16'

DN

DN

Photos on these pages by Jim Westphalen

"*It was the magnificence of [Connor Homes'] in-house construction facility that impressed me,' states [homeowner and engineer] Barbara. 'You could tell by the efficiency of its factory that precision was a primary objective.*"

"Brian's Song" by Stephen T. Spewock, New Old House, Spring 2009

TRADITIONAL STYLE CABINETS
with raised panels and beaded surrounds are included in the price of our cata-
log homes. Many custom options are available, as well as wooden countertops.
All cabinetry is made of local maple and handcrafted in our mill shops.

THE CEPHAS STEVENS HOUSE

1,904 Square Feet

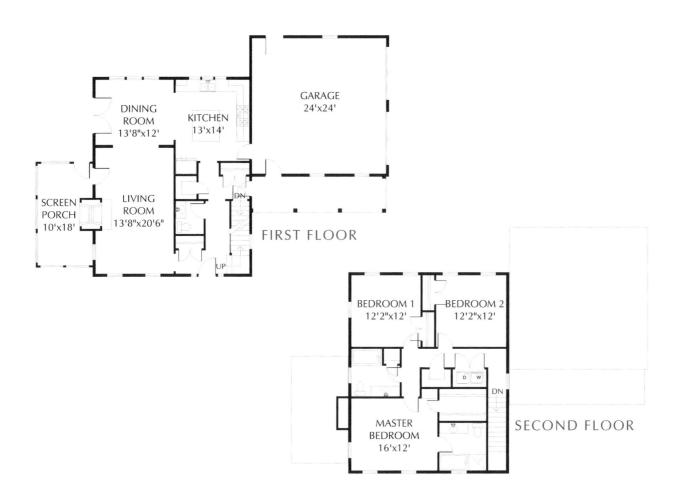

DINING ROOM 13'8"x12'

KITCHEN 13'x14'

GARAGE 24'x24'

SCREEN PORCH 10'x18'

LIVING ROOM 13'8"x20'6"

DN

UP

FIRST FLOOR

BEDROOM 1 12'2"x12'

BEDROOM 2 12'2"x12'

D W

DN

MASTER BEDROOM 16'x12'

SECOND FLOOR

THE TEAGUE JONES HOUSE

2,341 Square Feet

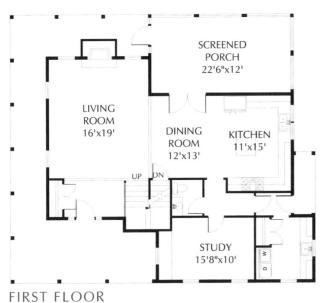

SCREENED
PORCH
22'6"x12'

LIVING
ROOM
16'x19'

DINING
ROOM
12'13'

KITCHEN
11'x15'

UP DN

STUDY
15'8"x10'

FIRST FLOOR

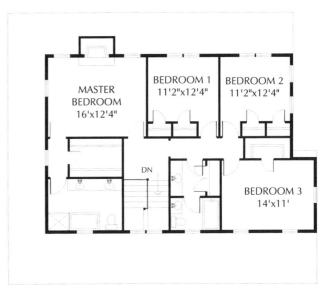

MASTER
BEDROOM
16'x12'4"

BEDROOM 1
11'2"x12'4"

BEDROOM 2
11'2"x12'4"

DN

BEDROOM 3
14'x11'

SECOND FLOOR

THE JESSE SHIELDS HOUSE

2,416 Square Feet

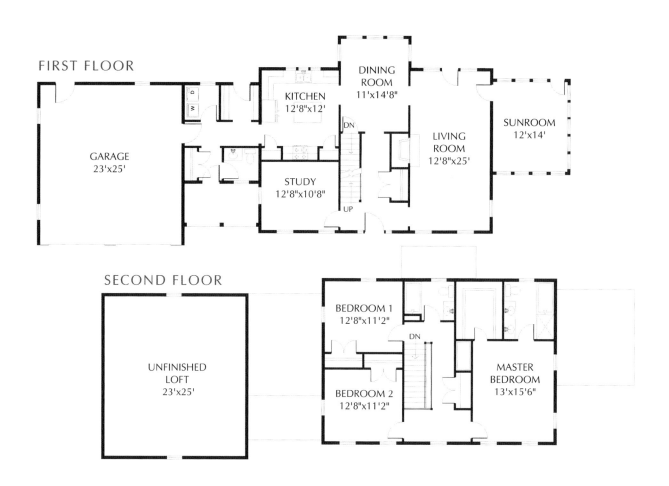

FIRST FLOOR

GARAGE
23'x25'

KITCHEN
12'8"x12'

DINING ROOM
11'x14'8"

SUNROOM
12'x14'

DN

STUDY
12'8"x10'8"

LIVING ROOM
12'8"x25'

UP

SECOND FLOOR

UNFINISHED LOFT
23'x25'

BEDROOM 1
12'8"x11'2"

DN

MASTER BEDROOM
13'x15'6"

BEDROOM 2
12'8"x11'2"

BELOW ARE JUST A FEW EXAMPLES of the ways that our customers have made a story-and-a-half Greek Revival home their own. As with any of the variations shown, you may contact us for floorplans and pricing.

The Enos Martin House does not have a mudroom, but has an extended garage with a loft above and a front porch.

The George Ellis House adds shutters and a cupola to make it appropriate for the Long Island coast, and a first floor guest room wing.

The Augustus Stebbins turned a garage wing into a large family room with a cathedral ceiling and has a first floor guest room.

THE CALEB NICKERSON HOUSE

3,192 Square Feet

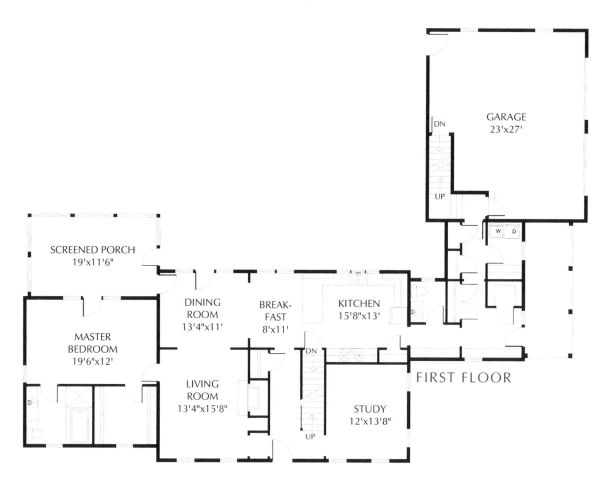

SCREENED PORCH
19'x11'6"

MASTER
BEDROOM
19'6"x12'

DINING
ROOM
13'4"x11'

BREAK-
FAST
8'x11'

KITCHEN
15'8"x13'

GARAGE
23'x27'

DN

UP

W D

LIVING
ROOM
13'4"x15'8"

DN

UP

STUDY
12'x13'8"

FIRST FLOOR

Photos on this page
by Jim Westphalen

GUEST SUITE
23'x19'

DN

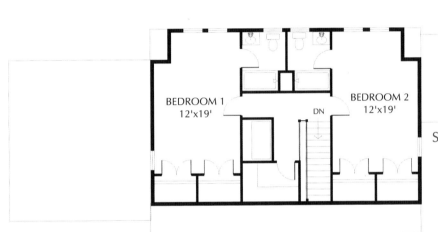

BEDROOM 1
12'x19'

DN

BEDROOM 2
12'x19'

SECOND FLOOR

FROM OUR CLIENTS

*"The finish materials are equally as
beautiful. As a designer, I know I
couldn't order cabinets and built-ins
for the cost of what Connor provides."*

Homeowner, Massachusetts

The Caleb Nickerson
mudroom bench featured
in New Old House, Spring 2011

THE HULL WALKER HOUSE

4,867 Square Feet

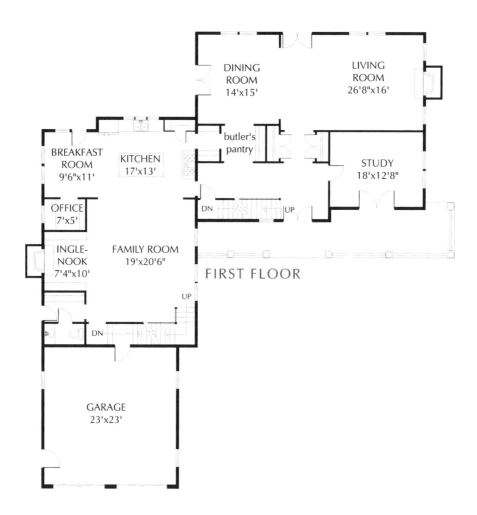

DINING ROOM
14'x15'

LIVING ROOM
26'8"x16'

butler's pantry

BREAKFAST ROOM
9'6"x11'

KITCHEN
17'x13'

STUDY
18'x12'8"

OFFICE
7'x5'

DN   UP

INGLE-NOOK
7'4"x10'

FAMILY ROOM
19'x20'6"

FIRST FLOOR

UP

DN

GARAGE
23'x23'

BEDROOM 2
12'x16'

MASTER
BEDROOM
16'x17'8"

BEDROOM 1
17'x12'

SITTING
ROOM
16'x11'

DN

W   D

BEDROOM 3
15'x14'6"

SECOND FLOOR

DN

BEDROOM 4
17'x18'

Photo by Jim Westphalen

THE EDSON MCDOWELL HOUSE

1,704 Square Feet

DINING
ROOM
12'x11'

KITCHEN
18'8"x12'4"

GARAGE
23'x23'

W   D

DN

LIVING
ROOM
12'x15'8"

STUDY
12'x11'

UP

FIRST FLOOR

BEDROOM 1
12'x19'

DN

BEDROOM 2
12'x19'

SECOND FLOOR

THE ALFRED STEVENS CARRIAGE HOUSE

1,720 Square Feet

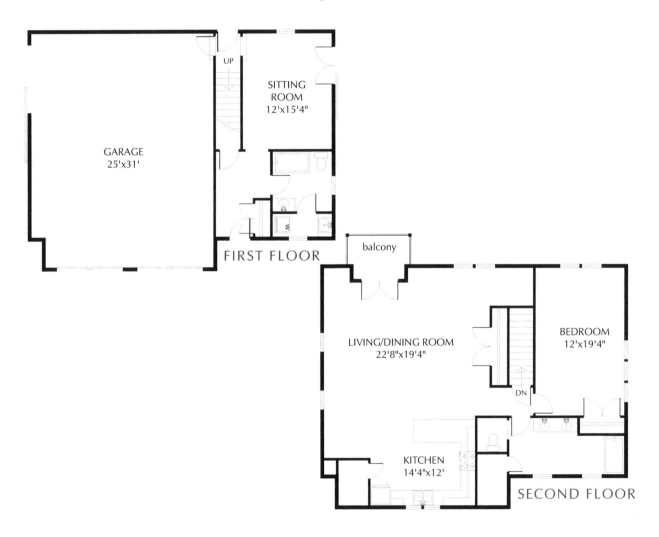

GARAGE
25'x31'

UP

SITTING
ROOM
12'x15'4"

FIRST FLOOR

balcony

LIVING/DINING ROOM
22'8"x19'4"

BEDROOM
12'x19'4"

DN

KITCHEN
14'4"x12'

SECOND FLOOR

THE SOLOMON BEAL HOUSE

5,201 Square Feet

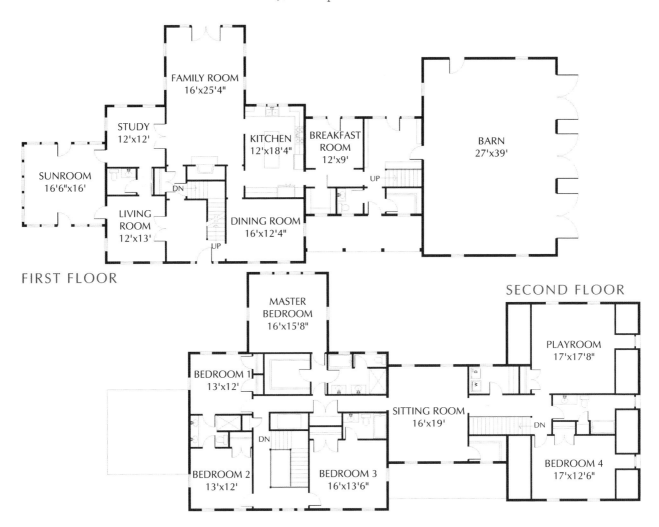

FIRST FLOOR

FAMILY ROOM
16'x25'4"

STUDY
12'x12'

KITCHEN
12'x18'4"

BREAKFAST
ROOM
12'x9'

BARN
27'x39'

SUNROOM
16'6"x16'

LIVING
ROOM
12'x13'

DINING ROOM
16'x12'4"

DN

UP

UP

SECOND FLOOR

MASTER
BEDROOM
16'x15'8"

PLAYROOM
17'x17'8"

BEDROOM 1
13'x12'

SITTING ROOM
16'x19'

BEDROOM 2
13'x12'

BEDROOM 3
16'x13'6"

BEDROOM 4
17'x12'6"

DN

DN

84

This exquisite paneled arch was fully built and assembled in the Connor Homes mill, and shipped in one piece to the jobsite.

Photo by Jim Westphalen

THE DUNCAN FENWICK HOUSE

3,876 Square Feet

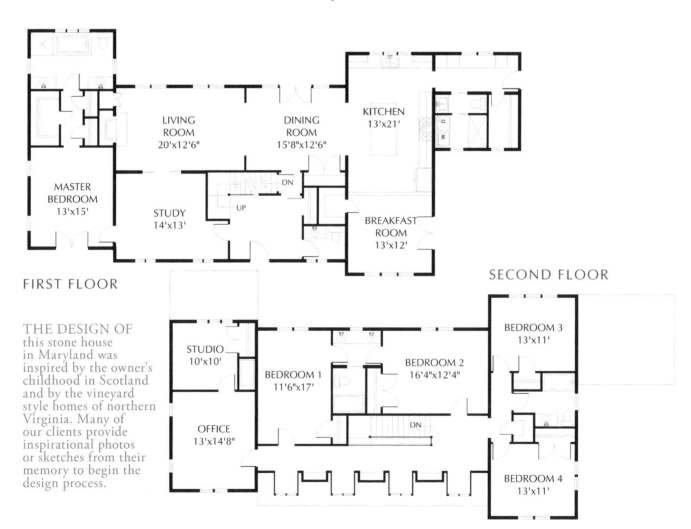

FIRST FLOOR

MASTER BEDROOM 13'x15'

LIVING ROOM 20'x12'6"

STUDY 14'x13'

UP

DN

DINING ROOM 15'8"x12'6"

KITCHEN 13'x21'

BREAKFAST ROOM 13'x12'

SECOND FLOOR

STUDIO 10'x10'

OFFICE 13'x14'8"

BEDROOM 1 11'6"x17'

BEDROOM 2 16'4"x12'4"

BEDROOM 3 13'x11'

DN

BEDROOM 4 13'x11'

THE DESIGN OF this stone house in Maryland was inspired by the owner's childhood in Scotland and by the vineyard style homes of northern Virginia. Many of our clients provide inspirational photos or sketches from their memory to begin the design process.

86

THE MEHITABLE ROBBINS HOUSE

2,192 Square Feet

GARAGE
23'x11'

KITCHEN
11'6"x12'

DINING/FAMILY ROOM
23'6"x12'

STORAGE
11'6"x13'

W
D

STUDY
11'4"x12'

DN

UP

LIVING
ROOM
11'x14'3"

BEDROOM 1
11'x12'2"

DN

MASTER
BEDROOM
10'8"x18'8"

BEDROOM 2
11'x12'2"

THE JOSEPHINE BALDWIN HOUSE

2,534 Square Feet

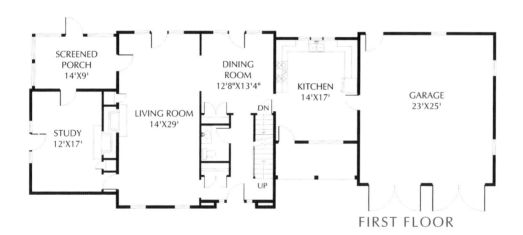

SCREENED PORCH
14'X9'

DINING ROOM
12'8"X13'4"

KITCHEN
14'X17'

GARAGE
23'X25'

LIVING ROOM
14'X29'

STUDY
12'X17'

DN

UP

FIRST FLOOR

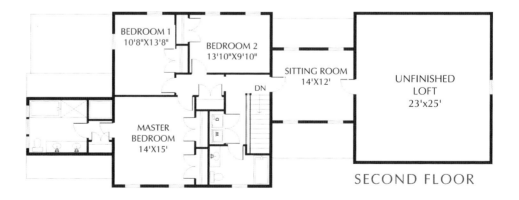

BEDROOM 1
10'8"X13'8"

BEDROOM 2
13'10"X9'10"

SITTING ROOM
14'X12'

UNFINISHED LOFT
23'x25'

DN

MASTER BEDROOM
14'X15'

SECOND FLOOR

Since the first Josephine Baldwin was built in 1988, it has been one of our most popular designs, and we have built variations for numerous families, from Virginia to New Hampshire.

"*The editors were very taken with Connor Homes, having mistaken one of their vernacular Greek Revival homes as a restored old house.*"

"Custom Build Authentic Designs"
Patricia Poore, Early Homes,
Summer 2008

THE HENRY COBB

2,650 Square Feet

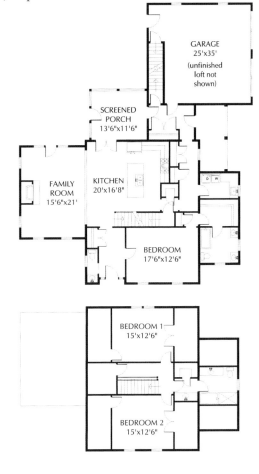

THE ROSE WETHERSFIELD

2,016 Square Feet

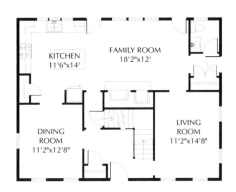

THE HELEN ALDRICH

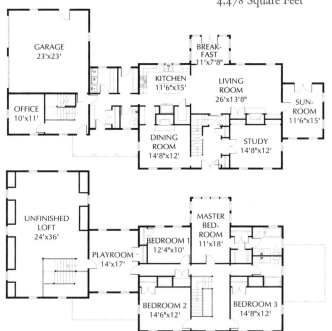

4,478 Square Feet

GARAGE 23'x23'

OFFICE 10'x11'

BREAK-FAST 11'x7'8"

KITCHEN 11'6"x15'

LIVING ROOM 26'x13'8"

SUN-ROOM 11'6"x15'

DINING ROOM 14'8"x12'

STUDY 14'8"x12'

UNFINISHED LOFT 24'x36'

PLAYROOM 14'x17'

MASTER BED-ROOM 11'x18'

BEDROOM 1 12'4"x10'

BEDROOM 2 14'6"x12'

BEDROOM 3 14'8"x12'

THE VIOLA BELL

2,480 Square Feet

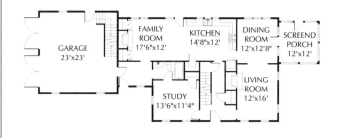

GARAGE 23'x23'

FAMILY ROOM 17'6"x12'

KITCHEN 14'8"x12'

DINING ROOM 12'x12'8"

SCREEND PORCH 12'x12'

STUDY 13'6"x11'4"

LIVING ROOM 12'x16'

UNFINISHED LOFT 23'x23'

BEDROOM 14'10"x12'

MASTER BEDROOM 13'6"x14'10"

BEDROOM 12'x14'4"

OUR ARCHITECTS frequently create new home designs. If you don't see what you are looking for in our catalog, talk to one of our Sales Associates: your perfect home may already have been designed!

two
COUNTRY HOUSE
COLLECTION

WINTERTHUR®

CONNOR HOMES WAS GRANTED THE EXCLUSIVE LICENSE to produce a line of homes endorsed by Winterthur: the museum, garden, and library that is the former home of Henry Francis du Pont. The design inspiration for this new line of historically authentic, architecturally detailed homes comes from the museum's extensive archives as well as interpretations and adaptations of existing architecture presently found on the Winterthur estate. Our architects are always adding new designs to this lovely collection.

THE GATE HOUSE

2,176 Square Feet

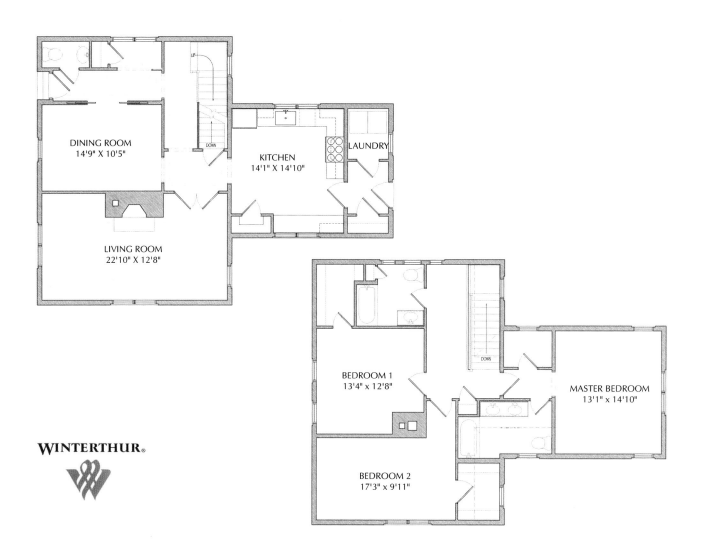

DINING ROOM
14'9" X 10'5"

KITCHEN
14'1" X 14'10"

LAUNDRY

LIVING ROOM
22'10" X 12'8"

BEDROOM 1
13'4" x 12'8"

MASTER BEDROOM
13'1" x 14'10"

BEDROOM 2
17'3" x 9'11"

UP

DOWN

DOWN

WINTERTHUR®

THE MORDINGTON HOUSE

1,950 Square Feet

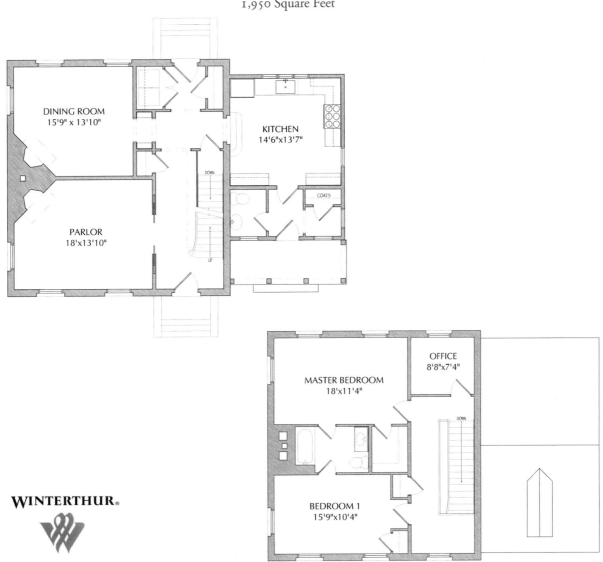

DINING ROOM
15'9" x 13'10"

KITCHEN
14'6"x13'7"

DOWN

COATS

PARLOR
18'x13'10"

MASTER BEDROOM
18'x11'4"

OFFICE
8'8"x7'4"

DOWN

BEDROOM 1
15'9"x10'4"

WINTERTHUR®

HAMPTON COURT
4,145 Square Feet

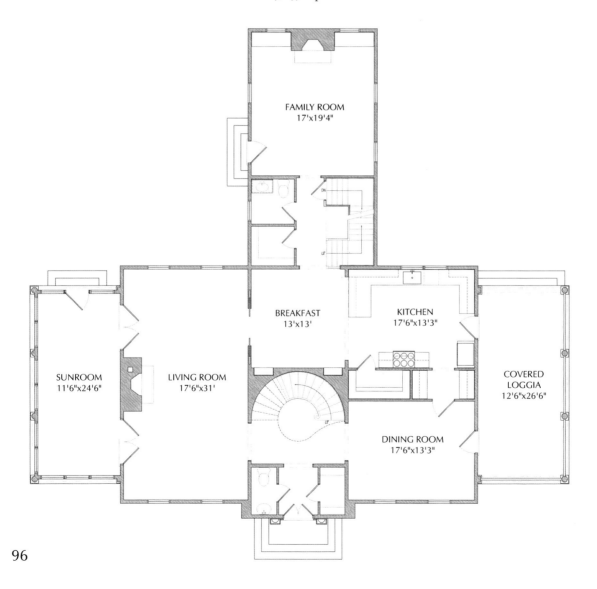

FAMILY ROOM
17'x19'4"

BREAKFAST
13'x13'

KITCHEN
17'6"x13'3"

SUNROOM
11'6"x24'6"

LIVING ROOM
17'6"x31'

COVERED
LOGGIA
12'6"x26'6"

DINING ROOM
17'6"x13'3"

BEDROOM 3
17'x12'8"

MASTER
BEDROOM
17'6"x13'

BEDROOM 1
13'8"x12'3"

BEDROOM 2
13'8"x12'3"

WINTERTHUR®

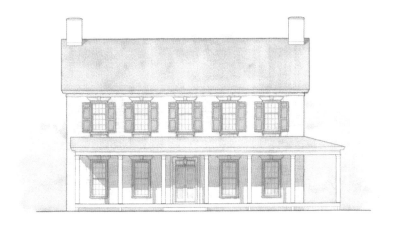

THE HOTTENSTEIN HOUSE

3,400 Square Feet

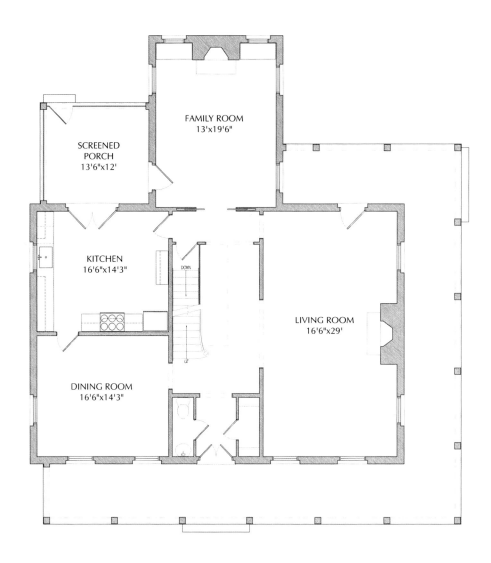

FAMILY ROOM
13'x19'6"

SCREENED
PORCH
13'6"x12'

KITCHEN
16'6"x14'3"

DOWN

LIVING ROOM
16'6"x29'

DINING ROOM
16'6"x14'3"

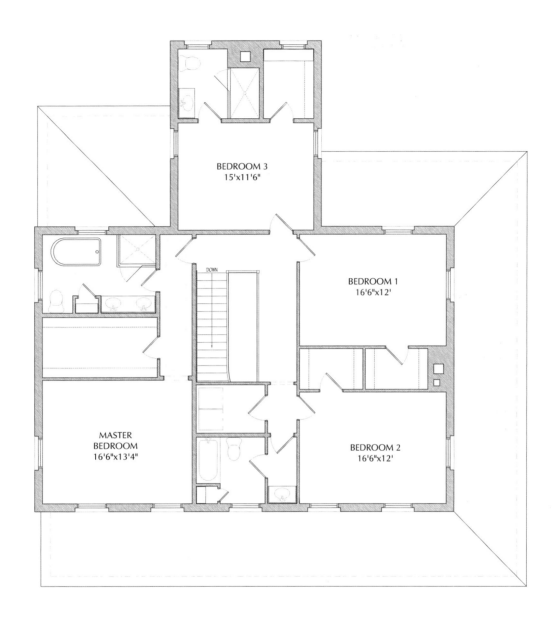

BEDROOM 3
15'x11'6"

DOWN

BEDROOM 1
16'6"x12'

MASTER
BEDROOM
16'6"x13'4"

BEDROOM 2
16'6"x12'

WINTERTHUR®

three
SIMPLE CLASSICS

Photos on these pages by Jim Westphalen

*W*E HAVE ALWAYS DESIGNED OUR HOMES WITH AN UNDERSTANDING that the more cost-efficient we make them, the more opportunities we have to build them. In the company's 42 years of building new old homes, the ability to keep new construction affordable has become more challenging each year as costs have risen. It has always been our goal to have homes that are affordable to a wide range of buyers from first-time homeowners to savvy repeat buyers.

In this line of homes we have taken some of our favorite smaller homes, retained the same beautiful exterior detailing found in our catalog homes and looked for ways to ensure they could be built in a range of $155-$175/per square foot, completed cost (excluding land and site specific work). We made sure the framing was simple, the layout efficient, the placement of windows and doors sensible, the materials durable and the design enduring.

These plans are presented and priced to be built exactly as shown with no modifications. The ability to repeat these homes for different homeowners throughout the country allows the design cost to be shared. Upon request these plans can be mirrored at no additional charge. Minor modifications can always be made by your on-site builder and we are happy to advise where we can.

Left, the front door of the Beatrice Bailey and right, the Margaret Cooley porch

THE SYBIL FELTON HOUSE

1,768 Square Feet

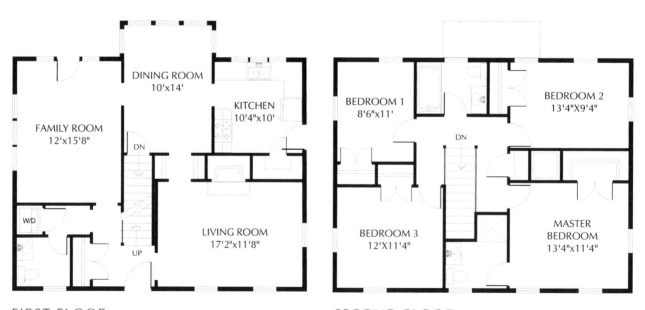

FAMILY ROOM
12'x15'8"

W/D

DINING ROOM
10'x14'

KITCHEN
10'4"x10'

DN

UP

LIVING ROOM
17'2"x11'8"

FIRST FLOOR

BEDROOM 1
8'6"x11'

BEDROOM 2
13'4"X9'4"

DN

BEDROOM 3
12'X11'4"

MASTER
BEDROOM
13'4"x11'4"

SECOND FLOOR

THE MARGARET COOLEY HOUSE

2,680 Square Feet

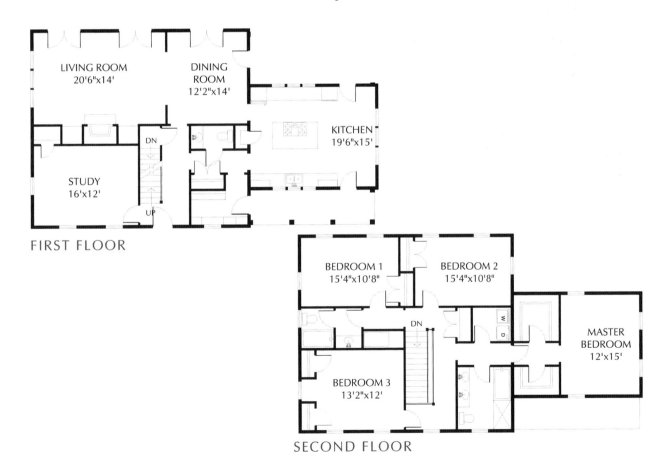

FIRST FLOOR

LIVING ROOM
20'6"x14'

DINING
ROOM
12'2"x14'

KITCHEN
19'6"x15'

DN

STUDY
16'x12'

UP

SECOND FLOOR

BEDROOM 1
15'4"x10'8"

BEDROOM 2
15'4"x10'8"

DN

MASTER
BEDROOM
12'x15'

BEDROOM 3
13'2"x12'

THE GILES HAMBLIN HOUSE

1,904 Square Feet

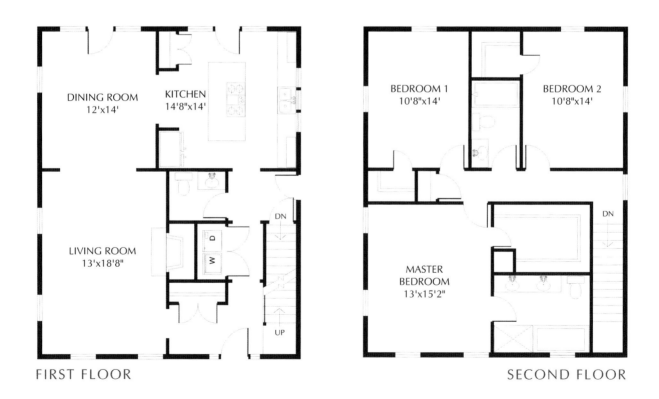

DINING ROOM
12'x14'

KITCHEN
14'8"x14'

LIVING ROOM
13'x18'8"

DN

W   D

UP

BEDROOM 1
10'8"x14'

BEDROOM 2
10'8"x14'

MASTER
BEDROOM
13'x15'2"

DN

FIRST FLOOR

SECOND FLOOR

Simple Classics: a recently completed Dorothy James, a Hope Concannon nearing completion, an Abigail Hallett for sale as a spec house, the porch and mudroom addition on the Dorothy James, a Giles Hamblin nearing completion, and a Margaret Cooley under construction. Since launching the collection in 2009, the Simple Classics have presented a valuable alternative for those on a tight timeline or tight budget, and the ideal package for a local general contractor to build as a spec house.

THE ELEAZOR DOUGHTY HOUSE

1,870 Square Feet

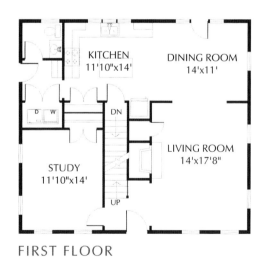

KITCHEN
11'10"x14'

DINING ROOM
14'x11'

D W

DN

STUDY
11'10"x14'

LIVING ROOM
14'x17'8"

UP

FIRST FLOOR

MASTER
BEDROOM
11'10"x18'8"

DN

BEDROOM 1
10'6"x11'

BEDROOM 2
10'6"x11'

SECOND FLOOR

THE ABIGAIL HALLETT HOUSE

2,012 Square Feet

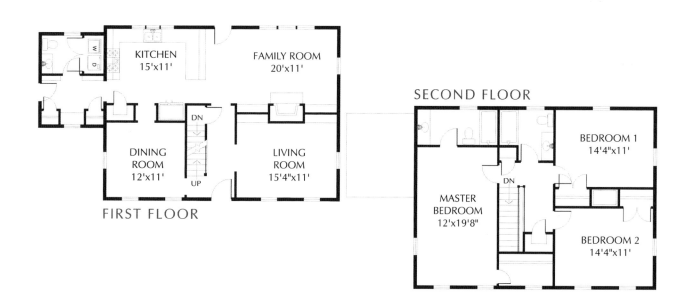

KITCHEN
15'x11'

FAMILY ROOM
20'x11'

SECOND FLOOR

DN

DINING
ROOM
12'x11'

LIVING
ROOM
15'4"x11'

BEDROOM 1
14'4"x11'

UP

DN

MASTER
BEDROOM
12'x19'8"

FIRST FLOOR

BEDROOM 2
14'4"x11'

THE DAMARIS EAMES HOUSE

2,022 Square Feet

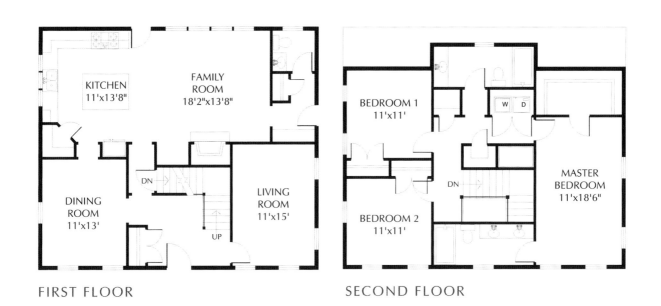

FIRST FLOOR

SECOND FLOOR

FROM OUR CLIENTS

"I had some time between jobs so I decided to build one of the Simple Classic Homes. The shell arrived less than a month after I ordered it and it went up wicked-fast - I had it framed in four days. If I had been impressed before, I was blown away with the actual product. I've been custom stick building for 30 years and there is no way I can build a house with the same quality of materials and the architectural detail as a Connor Home for anywhere close to the price. Apples to apples, stick building takes longer and is less profitable.

If I could say just one word about Connor Homes and their mill built kits it would be 'phenomenal'. I wish I'd done this five years ago."

Builder, Vermont

THE THOMAS LATHAM HOUSE

2,100 Square Feet

LIVING ROOM
13'x18'

DINING ROOM
11'x14'

KITCHEN
12'x14'

DN

STUDY
13'x11'8"

UP

W D

FIRST FLOOR

BEDROOM 1
11'x10'6"

BEDROOM 2
11'4"x10'6"

MASTER BEDROOM
13'x16'2"

DN

BEDROOM 3
11'4"x12'8"

SECOND FLOOR

THE OLIVE WHEATLEY HOUSE

2,054 Square Feet

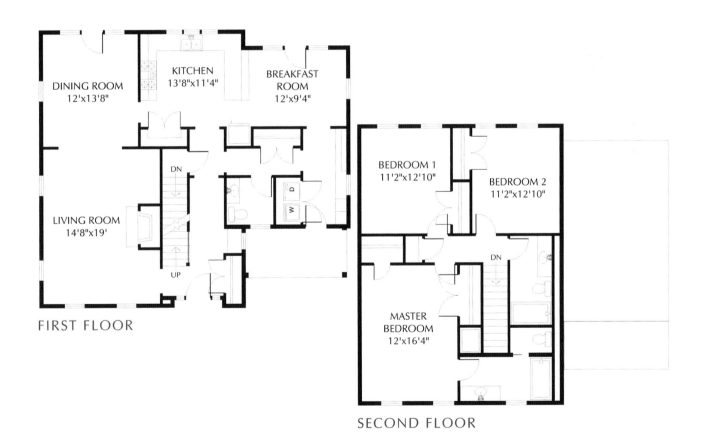

DINING ROOM
12'x13'8"

KITCHEN
13'8"x11'4"

BREAKFAST
ROOM
12'x9'4"

DN

LIVING ROOM
14'8"x19'

W   D

UP

FIRST FLOOR

BEDROOM 1
11'2"x12'10"

BEDROOM 2
11'2"x12'10"

DN

MASTER
BEDROOM
12'x16'4"

SECOND FLOOR

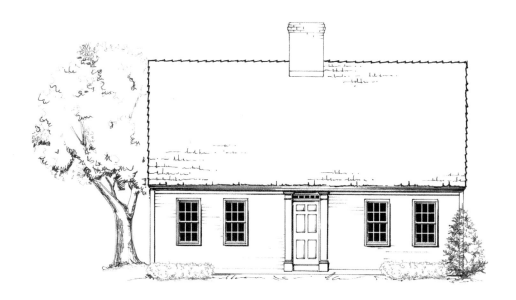

THE BEATRICE BAILEY HOUSE

1,974 Square Feet

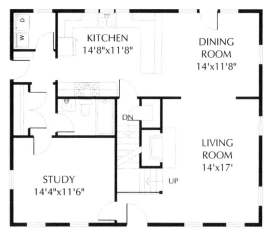

KITCHEN
14'8"x11'8"

DINING
ROOM
14'x11'8"

DN

UP

LIVING
ROOM
14'x17'

STUDY
14'4"x11'6"

FIRST FLOOR

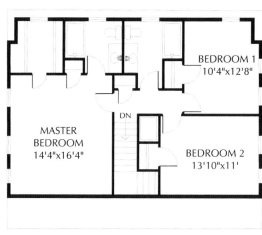

BEDROOM 1
10'4"x12'8"

DN

MASTER
BEDROOM
14'4"x16'4"

BEDROOM 2
13'10"x11'

SECOND FLOOR

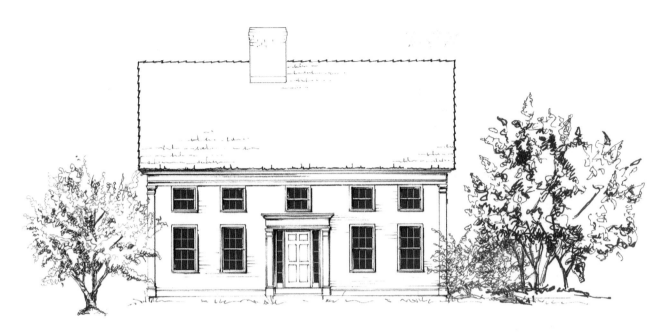

THE DOROTHY JAMES HOUSE

1,772 Square Feet

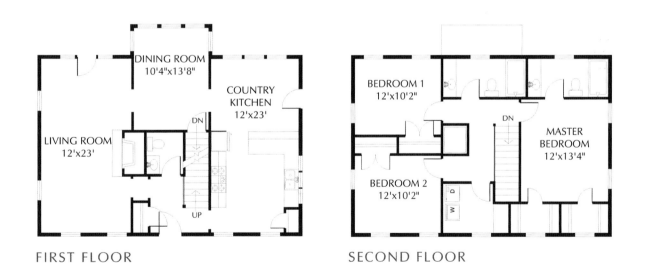

DINING ROOM
10'4"x13'8"

COUNTRY KITCHEN
12'x23'

DN

LIVING ROOM
12'x23'

UP

FIRST FLOOR

BEDROOM 1
12'x10'2"

DN

MASTER BEDROOM
12'x13'4"

BEDROOM 2
12'x10'2"

W D

SECOND FLOOR

THE HOPE CONCANNON HOUSE

1,568 Square Feet

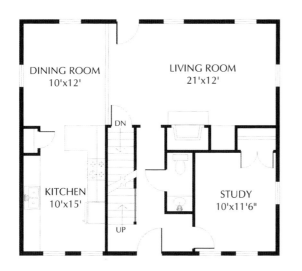

DINING ROOM
10'x12'

LIVING ROOM
21'x12'

DN

KITCHEN
10'x15'

STUDY
10'x11'6"

UP

FIRST FLOOR

MASTER
BEDROOM
10'x14'8"

BEDROOM 1
12'4"x10'2"

DN

W/D

BEDROOM 2
13'6"x10'2"

SECOND FLOOR

THE ALICE OLNEY HOUSE

1,772 Square Feet

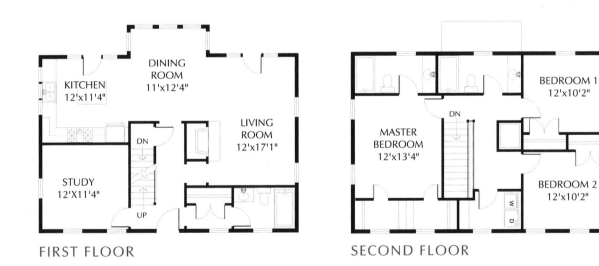

KITCHEN
12'x11'4"

DINING
ROOM
11'x12'4"

LIVING
ROOM
12'x17'1"

DN

STUDY
12'X11'4"

UP

FIRST FLOOR

MASTER
BEDROOM
12'x13'4"

DN

BEDROOM 1
12'x10'2"

BEDROOM 2
12'x10'2"

W
D

SECOND FLOOR

FROM OUR CLIENTS

"Within days of deciding which Simple Classic model to build, we had our plans submitted to our town's building department for permitting. Our building inspector approved the plans upon first review and we broke ground the following week. Our neighbors were astonished at how quickly we had a weather-tight shell erected on site: after the first delivery from Connor Homes we had all exterior work complete within just a few weeks.

The end result is a beautiful, energy efficient home that looks like it has been in the neighborhood for over 100 years. We are complimented on how great it looks all the time. Best of all, despite the fact that we built a new house in the midst of a down housing market, the house appraised for significantly more than the cost of construction."

Homeowners,
Hanover, New Hampshire

As a professional real estate appraiser, I am often asked to give my opinion in a tax grievance, wherein a homeowner feels his home is over-valued by the town lister. When I arrived at the house, I said to the homeowner: "This is a Connor Home, is it not?"
The homeowner looked at me, smiling, and asked: "I'm not getting my appraisal reduced, am I?"
I replied: "No."

An Appraiser's Story,
Vermont

SHAKER STYLE CABINETS

The newest style of Connor Homes' cabinets is clean, simple and elegant, and comes standard in all Simple Classics. All cabinetry is made of local maple and handcrafted in our mill shops.

THE JANE PEASLEE SIMPLE CLASSIC

1,548 square feet

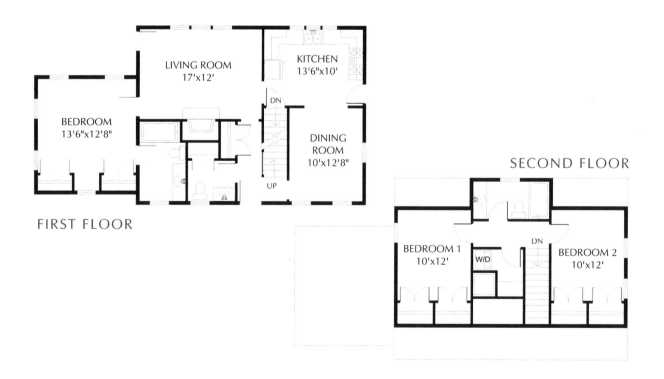

LIVING ROOM
17'x12'

KITCHEN
13'6"x10'

BEDROOM
13'6"x12'8"

DN

DINING
ROOM
10'x12'8"

UP

FIRST FLOOR

SECOND FLOOR

BEDROOM 1
10'x12'

W/D

DN

BEDROOM 2
10'x12'

THE BRAD STANDISH HOUSE

1,786 square feet

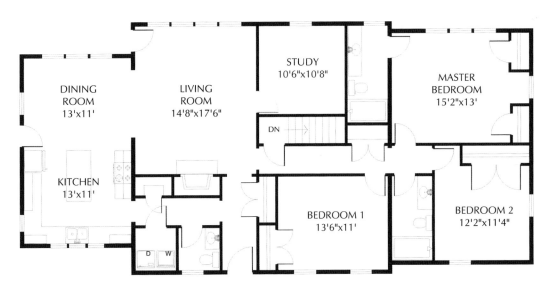

DINING
ROOM
13'x11'

LIVING
ROOM
14'8"x17'6"

STUDY
10'6"x10'8"

MASTER
BEDROOM
15'2"x13'

DN

KITCHEN
13'11'

BEDROOM 1
13'6"x11'

BEDROOM 2
12'2"x11'4"

D   W

FIRST FLOOR

four DESIGN SERVICES

the design process

If you have found Connor Homes, you already share our passion for classic American architecture, interpreted for the way we live today. We have spent our 40-plus years in the home building business researching, developing and improving our designs and building process, so that a Connor home is a result of combining superior design, skilled craftsmanship and modern technology that is unavailable elsewhere. For that reason, we do not design for anyone but our customers who have chosen us to craft their home in our mill-shops, and we never sell our designs to be built in any other way.

We have a choice of design fee structures that allows each customer to move at a comfortable pace. Our fees are pre-set, so there are no surprises. And since we both design and build the house, our design costs as a proportion of the whole project are much lower than those of an architectural firm, and because design is included in the package cost, customers enjoy the benefit of financing it with their mortgage, an option not available with conventional architectural design fees.

There are four phases of design, and they progress consecutively in the following order:

1. Schematic Design
2. Design Development
3. Production Documents
4. Interior Design

1. SCHEMATIC DESIGN PHASE

This is the start of the design process and typically begins with a personal meeting in our Vermont office or a conference call with one of our Project Designers. Customers can prepare for the first meeting by providing as much pertinent information as possible, including site plans, photos of the site, pictures of houses and architectural features they admire, and by completing our "Getting Started" questionnaire. A typical design session takes two to four hours. The project designer will need 10 to15 business days to complete the drawings and have the quotes prepared. The Schematic Design package can be presented as an email attachment, a fax or by mail at the convenience of the customer. The Schematic Design usually captures 90 - 95 % of the customer's goals for a new home.

This large, custom home near Old Chatham, New York was the result of a collaboration with the client's local architect.

The Henry Allerton House is a custom home on Lake Champlain, whose owners worked with our design staff to accomplish two primary goals: to "tell a story" with a mix of architectural styles from several periods, and to build as sustainably as possibly. The house is certified LEED Platinum.

2. DESIGN DEVELOPMENT

The complex process of design starts with the largest decisions: the shape and form of the house, placement and size of windows and doors, exterior trim, room layout and interior details.

The Design Development phase is a collaboration between you and your Project Designer that furthers the design work initiated in the Schematic Design phase. During this process, you may ask the Designer to show options for floor plans, exterior and interior details and materials, and these changes will be tracked on a "Quote Revision" sheet that allows you to review, accept or reject any changes along the way. The Design Development phase can take a few days to a few weeks. Once the design is complete, we will agree upon a production slot and a Contract will be prepared.

Then the finer details, such as the layout of the kitchen and the addition of personalized built-ins are considered in the Interior Design phase. We have found that customers find it easier to work through the details of the exterior and interior, including the interior trim and to complete these decisions, before moving on to the selection of kitchen and bath cabinetry and other design decisions such as custom built-ins. Those drawings will be completed during the Interior Design phase.

3. PRODUCTION DESIGN

The Production Design phase is an internal process to prepare the detailed construction documents and shop paperwork. We allow three weeks for this phase.

4. INTERIOR DESIGN

The Interior Designer begins the process with a personal meeting at our offices in Middlebury or a conference call. When complete, the interior drawings will include detailed drawings of the interior trim, millwork and cabinetry. During the process, you will be asked to finalize decisions concerning appliance and fixture selection, especially in the kitchen, before drawings can be finalized. The Interior Design process should take about three weeks for a catalog house to six weeks for a custom residence. Simple Classics are pre-designed, but custom millwork may be added and cabinetry modified under an hourly fee arrangement.

Top, a custom home in upstate New York; center, a custom shingled Georgian under construction in the Hamptons; and bottom, a custom primitive Colonial awaits a roof.

123

Photo by Jim Westphalen

Photo by Jim Westphalen

FROM COFFERED CEILINGS TO CURIO CABINETS, our interior design team will work with you to design gorgeous, functional and stylistically appropriate woodwork, which will be pre-built in our mills.

fees, agreements and payment schedules

There are two design fee structures at Connor Homes; the Design Retainer and the Deposit. Most customers start with a Design Retainer and progress to a Deposit, but clients may choose to proceed directly to Deposit on a home of their choice if there are only minor modifications to be made.

THE DESIGN RETAINER

For a modest fee, customers may have a one-time consultation with one of our Project Designers. The deliverable for this service is a complete Schematic Design drawing, including all four sides (elevations) of the house plan and scaled, labeled floor plans. In addition to quotes for the Connor Homes House Package, the Schematic Design includes a "Vital Statistics" report listing required quantities of some building materials not included in the Connor Homes' Package (such as paint and drywall) and estimated labor hours to erect and complete the customer's plan on site. Equipped with the Schematic Design package, a customer is in a position to request bids from General Contractors for the labor and materials cost to take their project from site preparation to moving day. The customer may proceed with the project by placing a Deposit, which begins the process of Design Development and Production Design. The one-time session with the Project Designer can take place at our Vermont location or by conference call.

The front and rear of the Matthew Endicott: a custom farmhouse in Ohio.

THERE ARE TWO LEVELS OF DESIGN RETAINER:

1. *Our customer starts with one of our Timeless Classics and makes modifications:*
    The Design Retainer is calculated by multiplying $2 times the square footage of the
    house plus any other added spaces such as barns and porches.
    For example, the Abigail Bearce House has 1,774 SF of finished living space plus 576 SF of
    garage: total gross square footage is 2,350 SF, so the Design Retainer is $4,700

2. *Our customer has a custom plan, wishes to develop a custom plan not based on one of the Timeless Classics*
    The Design Retainer is calculated by multiplying $2 times the square footage of the desired
    project size.
    For example, the customer plans a 2,500 square foot house with a 300 SF covered porch and
    a 600 SF garage: total gross square footage is 3,400 and the Design Retainer is $6,800.

The Design Retainer is 100% applicable to the purchase of the Connor Homes packages.

A complementary addition to a 200 year old brick home.

Photo by Jim Westphalen

A Perfect Match

WEDDING TWO CONSTRUCTION STYLES BEGINS AS A MARRIAGE OF CONVENIENCE, BUT THE END RESULT IS A PREFABRICATED ADDITION THAT TIES IN SEAMLESSLY WITH THIS RHODE ISLAND HOME.

FROM OUR CLIENTS

"'We got exactly what we wanted,' Cindy says. 'We added another house onto the existing house and tied them together. And it was fun!'"

"A Perfect Match" by Steve Cooper
Better Homes and Gardens,
February/March 2007

THE DEPOSIT

Once you have completed the Schematic Design under the Design Retainer process, you will have a quote for your Exterior Package and an estimate for your Interior Package from Connor Homes.

The Exterior Package Agreement requires a Deposit equal to 10% of the quote. The Deposit is required to become a client of record and to begin the process of fine-tuning the design, called the Design Development phase. The Deposit covers all subsequent design time and the preparation of plans required for permit application, construction documents and extra sets used by electrical and plumbing subcontractors as planning templates. The Deposit also guarantees the price for 120 days as well as a place in our production schedule. The deposit is non-refundable because failure to fill an assigned production slot is a significant lost opportunity cost for Connor Homes.

Customers may choose to place their deposits for their Exterior House Package and Interior House Package at the same time, or place just the Exterior House Package Deposit, complete the Design Development phase and then begin the Interior Design phase with their Interior Deposit.

The 14 Simple Classics are the only Connor Homes house plans that are pre-drawn. Since the drawings are complete and cannot be changed, there is no Schematic Design phase required and customers simply progress to the Deposit phase.

THE EXTERIOR PACKAGE & INTERIOR PACKAGE CONTRACTS

Once the Design Development Phase is complete Connor Homes will prepare the Exterior House Package Contract. There is a House Package Contract and an Interior Contract, each with its own set of drawings and other documentation.

The Exterior Package Contract will state the final package price and show the payments made to date, from the Design Retainer (if any) and the Deposit fee. The balance will be divided into two scheduled payments for the two deliveries that are typically required to fulfill the Contract. The first delivery is the framing package and the second delivery is the exterior trim kit which includes windows, doors, roofing, siding and pre-built and running architectural trim. For the Interior Contract, the first delivery includes everything but cabinetry and the second delivery is the custom cabinetry.

PAYMENT SCHEDULE

Payments are due when each portion of the package is in production in our millshops on the Contract dates, irrespective of when the actual delivery is made.

The payment amounts for each Contract break down in approximately this proportion:

    Payment One: 10% Deposit
    Payment Two: 60% of final package price
    Payment Three: 30% of final package price

Feel free to call or write with further questions.

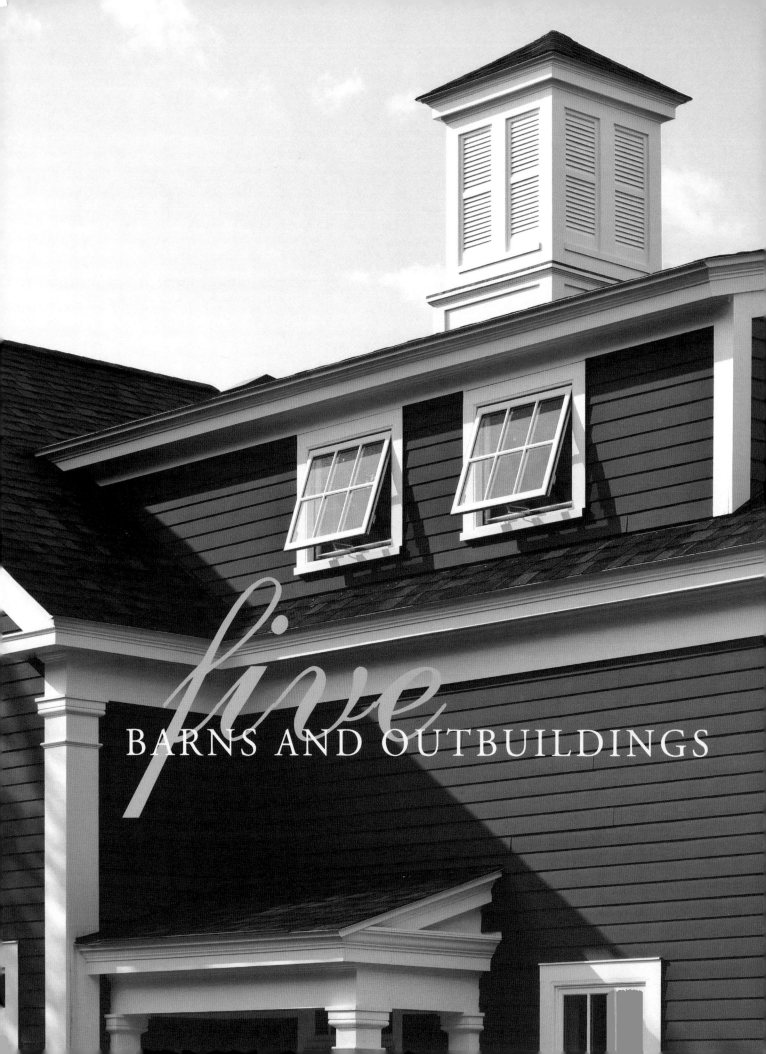

five
BARNS AND OUTBUILDINGS

THE BARNS AND OUTBUILDINGS OF AN EARLIER ERA would have been designed and built for purposes no longer needed. However, the architecture of these earlier buildings can still be copied and reproduced on the exterior, while adapting their interiors to new uses such as garages, garden sheds and general storage. Of course, sometimes we still build barns and stables to be barns and stables!

Many of our customers merely want to house their automobiles in a garage that doesn't look like one. Others want a true carriage house with actual living quarters, and still others want an entire house that looks like a converted barn. Our diverse knowledge of historic architectural barn styles enables us to accomplish all of these goals with efficiency and taste.

Each of the barns shown in this section can be built as is, or modified. A design retainer allows each customer to work with a project designer to modify an existing design, or design a custom plan.

Photos on these pages by Jim Westphalen

129

THE CHIMNEY POINT BARN

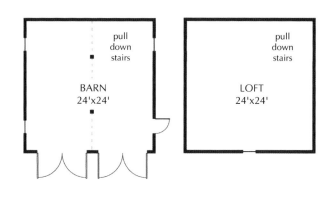

pull down stairs

BARN
24'x24'

pull down stairs

LOFT
24'x24'

THE SAWYER BAY BARN

BARN
30'x24'

THE CONNECTICUT RIVER BARN

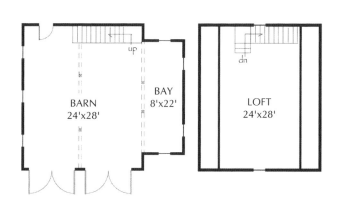

up

BARN
24'x28'

BAY
8'x22'

dn

LOFT
24'x28'

THE McNEIL COVE BOATHOUSE

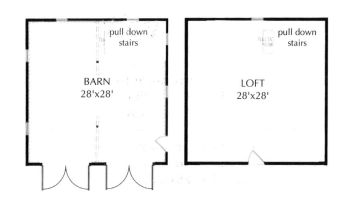

BARN
28'x28'

pull down
stairs

LOFT
28'x28'

pull down
stairs

THE GLOUCESTER BARN

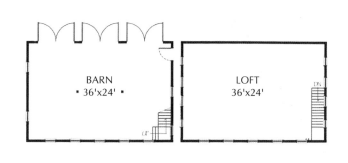

BARN
36'x24'

LOFT
36'x24'

THE GREEN MOUNTAIN BARN

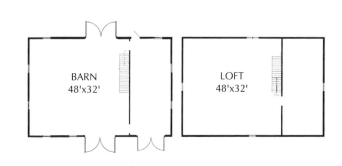

BARN
48'x32'

LOFT
48'x32'

THE JOHNS RIVER BARN

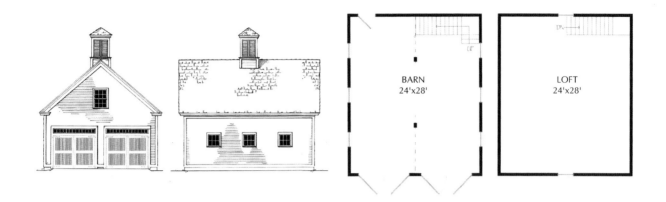

BARN
24'x28'

LOFT
24'x28'

THE DOG TEAM BARN

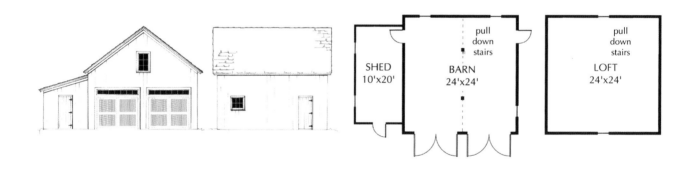

SHED
10'x20'

pull
down
stairs

BARN
24'x24'

pull
down
stairs

LOFT
24'x24'

THE HARTFORD BARN

BARN
24'x36'

LOFT
24'x36'

THE WEST ADDISON BARN

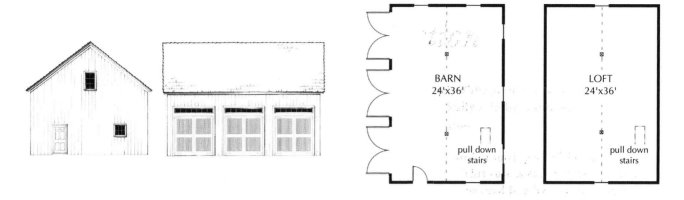

BARN
24'x36'

pull down
stairs

LOFT
24'x36'

pull down
stairs

THE LOUDOUN COUNTY BARN

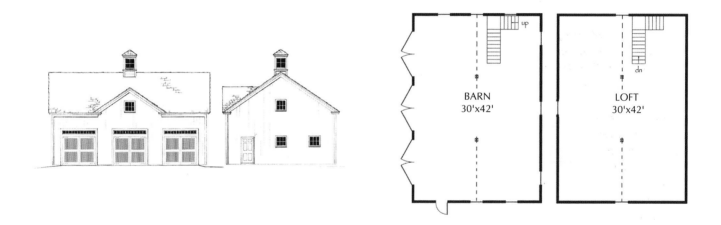

up

BARN
30'x42'

dn

LOFT
30'x42'

THE BABB CREEK LIVESTOCK BARN

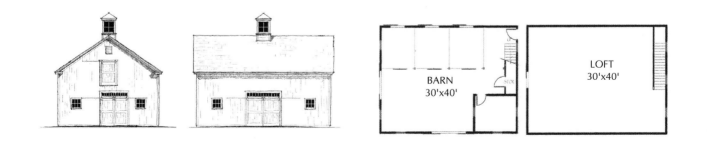

BARN
30'x40'

LOFT
30'x40'

THE BORDEN POND CARRIAGE HOUSE

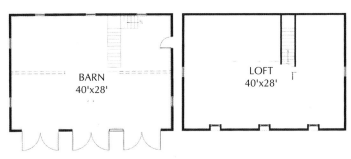

BARN
40'x28'

LOFT
40'x28'

THE BROOKFIELD GUEST BARN

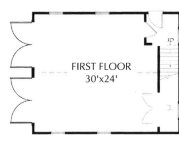

FIRST FLOOR
30'x24'

APARTMENT
30'x24'

THE MENDON PEAK POOLHOUSE

EQUIPMENT ROOM

SHOWER

KITCHEN

BATH

COVERED PORCH

THE CRANE LAKE CARRIAGE HOUSE

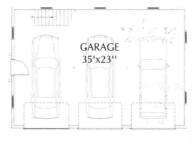

GARAGE
35'x23''

BATH
6'x7'

LIVING
ROOM
18'x11'
KITCHEN
17'x9'

BED-
ROOM
10'X12'

THE CEDAR POINT CARRIAGE HOUSE

BARN
35'x30'

LOFT
35'x30'

THE BEEBE HILL BARN

OFFICE
13'x19'

GARAGE
25'10"x28'

STUDIO
32'x26'

THE SNAKE MOUNTAIN HORSE BARN

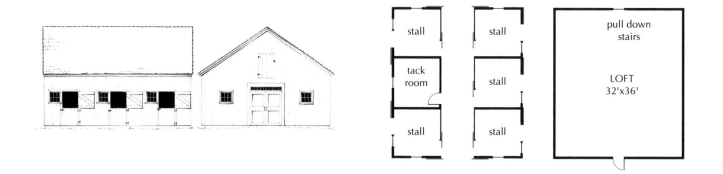

THE WOODSTOCK BARN

THE KINGSMILL HORSE BARN

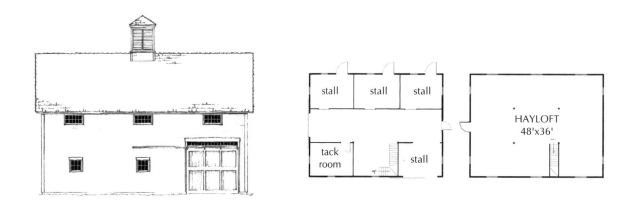

THE TREMONT CARRIAGE HOUSE

THE KETCHAM HILL BARN

THE WALKER BARN

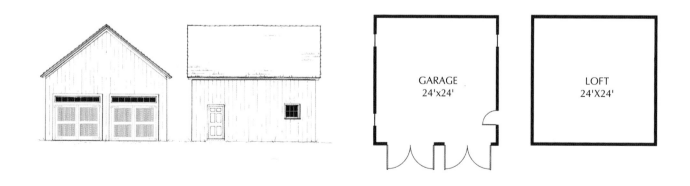

THE COOLEY CARRIAGE BARN

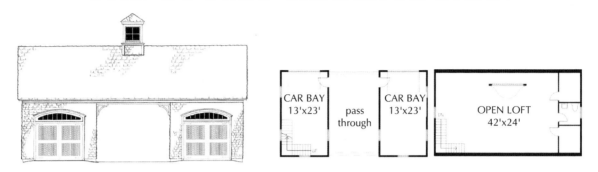

| CAR BAY 13'x23' | pass through | CAR BAY 13'x23' | OPEN LOFT 42'x24' |

THE CORNWALL POOLHOUSE

| CHANGING ROOM 28'x18' | LOFT 28'x18' |

CUPOLA OPTIONS

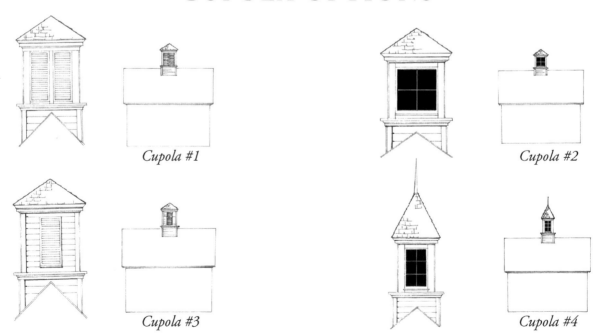

Cupola #1

Cupola #2

Cupola #3

Cupola #4

Photos on this page by Jim Westphalen

139

Photo by Jim Westphalen

materials and specifications

Our home packages contain the design and materials for the creation of your very own new old home. We have chosen to focus on the portions of your home that will bring the most value in the design and execution of a new old home and best utilize the years of experience found at Connor Homes.

We include:

- Design, building plans and material specifications
- Exterior framing components
- Exterior trim, assembled trim elements
- Windows, doors, roofing and siding materials
- Interior trim, flooring, stairs and cabinetry

Other portions of the building timeline will be coordinated and handled by your builder such as site work, foundation, on-site erection labor, masonry, plumbing, heating, electrical, insulation, sheetrock and miscellaneous other subcontractors and finishing materials not included in our package.

EXTERIOR PACKAGE MATERIALS

We choose our Exterior Package materials based on their ability to stand the test of time, replicate authentic aesthetics of earlier homes and provide practical price points that keep these homes affordable.

Our catalog prices include as standard:

• Exterior Shell Envelope: sills & sill sealer, girder(s), wood and steel bearing posts, pre-cut floor systems, cross bridging, blocking, metal hangers, 3/4" T&G fir plywood floor sheathing, panelized 2x6 exterior walls with 1/2" fir plywood applied, panelized interior walls, insulation for enclosed corners, top plates, 2x4 bracing, sheetrock nailers, Raindrop® house wrap, pre-cut rafters, 1/2" fir plywood roof sheathing, 30# roofing felt, hurricane straps, rafter ties, pre-built rake ladders, ice & water shield per plans and adhesives as required.

• Exterior trim: (All exterior trim and architectural details are primed, backprimed and Borate-treated WindsorONE™ pine exterior trim, with an option for primed solid wood cypress trim.) Pre-built returns with pre-bent flashing, eave and cornice trim, gable rake trim, pre-built corner boards and entry systems, pre-bent copper flashing for entry and window heads, drip cap, gable ornament if shown, pre-built pediments and window heads if shown, soffit vent and gable vents.

• Also included are Green Mountain Window Milestone™ series simulated divided lite windows, krypton or argon-filled insulated glass with low-e coating, applied 5/4 x 4 exterior casings and 2" historic sill in a factory-primed wood exterior and natural interior, Simpson Performance Series® fir wood doors with mahogany thresholds, simulated divided lite insulated glass doors, oil-rubbed bronze Emtek® door hardware and insulated transoms and sidelites per plans.

•Exterior Finishes include a red cedar shingle roof, cedar breather, vertical grain hemlock pre-primed clapboards, natural vertical board shiplap pine barn siding if applicable, adhesives and painted coil stock flashing. Additionally, if shown in the plan, we provide pre-cut porches, screen porches and decks with pre-cut pressure treated joists, rafters and support systems, pre-built porch posts, mangaris wood decking, and 1x6 double beaded pine ceilings. If shown in the elevations we also provide pre-built cupolas and louvered primed shutters with pintle hinges.

•This price includes detailed construction documents, and technical support. Custom structural design, engineering, lighting design and stamping of plans are available with additional fees.

ALTERNATIVE EXTERIOR MATERIAL OPTIONS:

IKO architectural asphalt roof shingles
Red or white cedar shingles
Copper flashing throughout
Custom plantation mahogany, or other wood species, carriage doors with operators
Cement board siding primed, or pre-painted
Solid stock cedar, Spanish cedar, mahogany, solid pine, or solid primed cypress exterior trim
Custom moulding profiles
Addition or deletion of shutters
Exterior lighting fixtures

INTERIOR PACKAGE MATERIALS

We include the following:

• Interior Trim: six-panel solid pine doors set in pine jambs, Emtek® oil-rubbed bronze hardware, select poplar 1x4 door trim with bead for doors and cased openings (nominally-cut and bundled for each door and opening), select poplar 1x4 trim and 3/8" bead, 1x5 bullnose sill and 1x4 apron for all windows (pre-cut to length and bundled for each window), select poplar 1x6 baseboard with milled top edge bead (nominally-cut and bundled for each room), 8009 crown moulding for first floor (nominally-cut and bundled for each first floor room), and wood closet shelving and rods with hardware (nominally-cut and pre-bundled for each closet or pantry)

• Stairs & Flooring: basement stairs (2x10 spruce stringers, closed risers, rail one-side), secondary stairs to attic or garage loft if shown in plans, main stairs (oak treads and nosing, poplar risers and stringers, maple newels and railings, primed balusters, and recessed panel wall under exposed stair wall) and wide pine flooring, 10", 12" and 14" throughout, construction adhesive and square head nails

• Millwork: all fireplace mantel(s) are included per plan as well as additional built-ins if identified in the pricing description

• Cabinetry: painted local sugar maple kitchen cabinets (raised panel, beaded inset flush door, dove-tailed drawers, full-extension, self-closing drawer glides and porcelain knobs), and painted local sugar maple bathroom vanities (to match kitchen cabinet specs)

• This price includes detailed construction documents and technical support.

INTERIOR MATERIAL OPTIONS:

Kitchen cabinets and vanities are available in lacquered cherry
or other wood species upon request.
They are also available with glass doors and cabinet amenities
such as roll-outs, lazy susans, utensil drawers, spice racks, etc.
Shaker style cabinets
15-lite interior doors
Glass transoms over interior doors
Alternative stair designs
Wainscoting, chair rail, raised panel walls
Specialty cabinets, bookcases, entertainment centers, built-in hutch units
Tub and spa surrounds
Benches, coat racks, window seats
Built-ins and/or specialties upon request

simple classics material specifications

EXTERIOR MATERIALS

All 16 inch-on-center SPF framing, 2x6 walls, panelized with pre-cut floors and fir plywood. Primed and back-primed Borate treated Windsor-ONE™ pine pre-built exterior trim. Green Mountain SDL argon insulated windows. Simpson Performance Series® wood exterior doors. Vertical grain primed hemlock clapboard, IKO 30-year architectural asphalt roof (wood available as upgrade). All miscellaneous materials to assemble package. Drawings included.

INTERIOR MATERIALS

Six panel moulded wood fiber doors set in jambs with Schlage oil-rubbed bronze hardware. Select poplar trim for windows, doors, baseboard and cased openings. Closet, pantry and linen shelving. One set finished stairs and one set basement stairs. Wide pine flooring in living, dining, foyer and study areas. Connor Homes traditional mantel. All miscellaneous materials to assemble package. Drawings included.

CABINETRY MATERIALS

Connor Homes Shaker style Cabinets for kitchen and baths as shown. Painted local maple cabinets with flat panels, inset flush doors, dovetailed drawers, full extension slides and painted wooden knobs. All miscellaneous materials to assemble package. Drawings included.

The front door of the Abigail Hallett, a Beatrice Bailey capped newel post, and a Shaker cabinet awaiting paint in our mill

144

seven

FREQUENTLY ASKED QUESTIONS

costs and pricing

What does it cost to build the entire home from start to finish including my builder's costs? In general, builders in Northern New England are building our houses from foundation through finish for $175-$250 per square foot, and the Simple Classics for $150-$185 per square foot, including our package price, with average demands and nice amenities. While builder costs can vary from state to state, we can help estimate the total cost for your home by providing you with a full budget estimate that includes costs for everything from foundation to finish painting. There are many factors that affect total costs such as site conditions, types of heating and plumbing systems chosen and level of interior finish desired. Connor Homes also has a field crew that is available to erect your home and help control costs.

How do you calculate square footage listed in the catalog? We calculate square footage as the livable finished space only. Additional spaces such as garages, porches, and unheated storage areas are not included in the listed square price but must be considered when tallying overall building costs.

How much is the initial deposit? The initial deposit is 10% of the shell package price. Your deposit gives you a place in our schedule, and guarantees the quoted shell package price for the building season.

How can I get a realistic price for the total project? We recommend that you enlist a builder as early on as possible to help develop a budget for your project. We provide "Vital Statistics" on the complete construction of your home package to aid your builder in putting an estimate together early in the process. We use our years of experience as general contractors to help you develop a realistic total budget, but costs vary from region to region and a local builder will best know realistic prices. We welcome direct calls from any builder you may be considering, and are happy to talk to him/her about what they can expect from Connor Homes.

Can you recommend a builder? We have a number of Preferred Builders who have worked with us on previous projects. You can find contact information on our website or call us for a referral. We also recommend that you talk to neighbors, family or friends in your area to find a good match. Or, our own Field Crew is available to complete the shell of our house.

I don't see a plan that meets my needs. How easy is it to make changes? We are happy to work with you to make changes to one of our catalog homes (with the exception of the Simple Classics which are designed to be built as shown), or to design a custom home. See our chapter on "Design Services" to learn more.

How can I convey my changes or ideas to Connor Homes? Each client who has placed a Design Retainer or Deposit will be assigned a project architect who will be in touch via phone, email, fax and/or mail to work with you on your plans. You may want to bring or send sketches, photographs, magazine tear-outs or any other information that you think will help demonstrate your wishes.

I don't see the style of home in your catalog that would be appropriate for my area. Do you build other regional vernaculars? For vernaculars or styles not found in our catalog we are happy to work directly with you. We have a talented design team with experience in vernaculars such as Southern Colonial, Craftsman/Bungalow, Colonial Revival, Mid-Atlantic Styles, Shingle Style and others. To initiate such a project we can schedule a time to meet or talk on the phone and the placement of a Design Retainer is all you need to get started.

Do you have plans not shown in your catalog to choose from? We are always customizing existing plans and designing new homes. Let us know what you are looking for and we may have a plan that fits your description that we can send to you.

What if I have my own architect or already have plans? We enjoy working with other architects, and can involve them during the design phase, or we can provide quotes and build from their plans, with proper permission. Additionally, architects who work with clients who are interested in historic designs are happy to work with us as they know that we can properly produce the kind of architectural details that their clients want.

How soon can I expect to receive drawings after I make my deposit? Typically, you will receive a preliminary set of floor plans, elevations and quotes from us within three or four weeks upon deposit. We will make changes as you need to these plans and revise your drawings until you are completely satisfied. When you sign off on these plans, we can begin the full set of construction drawings. See our chapter on "Design Services" for more detailed information on this process.

What are the ceiling heights in your homes? Ceiling heights vary from 7'1/2" feet to 12' or more and are a function of each design style.

What if I want a shorter or taller ceiling height? We can accommodate different ceiling heights upon request, with the exception of the Simple Classics. We address each house specifically to ensure the scale and proportions of the home will be appropriate.

My local building department tells me that I need "stamped" plans to submit for approval. Do you provide me with "stamped" plans? Our plans are drawn to meet or exceed most national building codes. Local code requirements can vary greatly, so you will need to have our plans reviewed by a local architect or engineer, for local code compliance. You may choose to hire a local architect/engineer to "stamp" our plans indicating that they are in compliance with local codes. We can provide stamped plans for an additional fee.

What about my mechanical and electrical plans? Mechanical and electrical plans are not included in our set of drawings. These plans are typically provided by your local mechanical and electrical subcontractor, or are drawn by a qualified mechanical/electrical engineer. We will gladly provide you with additional sets of floor plans and sections that your local mechanical/electrical designer can use as a template at no extra charge.

delivery, schedule and production

How far from your manufacturing facility will you deliver a house package? While most of our homes are shipped within the Northeast, we can and do deliver around the world! While we typically ship by truck, we can work with you to determine the most efficient and cost effective method of shipment to you.

Doesn't it cost more to deliver to a further destination? Yes, but the freight cost is a small part of the overall house cost, so even the additional freight for extra long distance is still cost effective. This cost is easily offset by the savings in labor over a site built house, along with the many other efficiencies to be realized in a factory prebuilt home.

What is the lead time for delivery of a house package to my site? Lead time varies depending on time of year, drafting requirements, and complexity and size of the house, but averages about 6-8 weeks in summer and fall and 4-6 weeks in winter and spring from the time of plan acceptance. When we receive your deposit, we will assign a delivery date as close as possible to your requested delivery date. However, knowing the vagaries of weather, permitting, and financing, we will work closely with you to adjust the delivery date to accommodate your progress in these areas.

Who puts the shell package together when it arrives at my site? You will need a local contractor or the Connor Homes Field Crew (unless you are serving as your own general contractor and builder) to erect our shell package. We can often recommend a local contractor for you. If your builder is not familiar with panelized construction we can arrange to have a company representative meet your new builder on-site at the first delivery.

Do all the materials come at once? No. We will deliver the house in stages so that you will have minimal storage requirements at your site. Should you wish to have all the materials delivered at once, and have storage available on site, we are happy to accommodate you.

What kind of support materials come with the house to assist me or my builder? In addition to the "Builder's Guide", you will receive a highly detailed set of drawings that include foundation plan, floor plans, sections, rafter plans, floor joists layouts, elevations, and more. Also, because our trim detailing is so important to our homes, we include details of all cornice work, and any other architectural details that pertain to your house.

materials and specifications

I notice that you use vertical grain hemlock primed and backprimed clapboard. I've been told that cedar clapboards are superior because they are more rot resistant. Why is hemlock used instead of cedar? We use primed and backprimed hemlock because most of our customers intend to paint their houses, and hemlock is far superior to cedar in holding paint. Furthermore, the tannin in cedar bleeds through the surface for many years, and will stain a light colored finish. It is a common misconception that cedar is the only choice for wood siding, when the species of wood is not nearly as important as the manner in which it is milled. Vertical grain or quarter sawn milling is the only acceptable manner in which a clapboard should be sawn, because it yields a product that can withstand the seasonal expansion and contraction that is inevitable in climates like the Northeast. While it is true that cedar is more rot resistant than other softwoods, this is a moot point, as clapboard failure is more commonly the result of cupping and splitting, which is unavoidable in any species of clapboard that is not milled with the vertical grained method. Vertical grained clapboards in softwoods other than cedar have been known to last well over a hundred years without failure, and indeed are what are found on historic houses of this area, as red cedar is not native to the Northeast. For those customers planning to stain their homes in the red/brown family, cedar is still an option, and is about the same cost as the primed hemlock. We also offer a natural cedar shingle for siding for about the same cost as well.

What can I expect in terms of longevity for the red cedar roofs that are standard with your houses? We use a red cedar wood shingle which is a very authentic looking roof that has been used quite extensively in historic home renovations and has a life expectancy of 40 years or more. Of course, we offer other roofing choices such as architectural asphalt and standing seam metal.

Can I make changes to the standard materials and specifications in your house packages? Yes. We offer many options to the materials listed in our standard specifications; you will find some of them listed in the chapter "Materials and Specifications." The materials that are standard in our packages have been chosen after years of research and experience to provide the greatest quality and durability, maintain our high architectural standards, and to minimize our impact on the environment. We have designed homes for clients with chemical sensitivity that use low or no off-gassing materials, or for clients who simply wish to live more sustainably, or for clients living in unique climates, and we can help advise you on the appropriate materials for your home style, region and sustainability goals. Feel free to call or email us to inquire about a material you may not see listed.

What kind of framing lumber is used in the construction of a Connor Home, and what are the design criteria? We use kiln dried lumber for all studs, floor joists and rafters, because it is known for its strength and resistance to warpage. Like the historic houses that we replicate, we intend that our homes will last for hundreds of years and be passed on from generation to generation. For this reason we use only top quality materials in our homes, and use strict design criteria intended to enable our homes to withstand the rigors of the Northeast climate. Our exterior walls are 2x6, 16" on center, we use rafters, not trusses, and all our sheathing is fir plywood, not composite sheathing.

Your specifications call for simulated divided lite windows, but I have heard the authentic divided lite windows are more traditional for a reproduction home. What is the difference? There are so many window manufacturers, offering so many options, that this may be one of the most confusing issues in a new home. In spite of the many choices offered, windows can be classified into three basic categories. The first is authentic divided lite windows. This is the least sophisticated, but most closely mimics an historic window sash, (as it consists of a piece of glass puttied into muntin bars, the wood dividers). In order to give this type of window a creditable energy rating, a second layer of glass is added. This second layer is in the form of either a storm window, or

an applied energy panel, both using low "e" glass to increase energy efficiency. Since most people do not wish to struggle with the seasonal task of changing storm windows, they opt for the applied energy panel. This serves the same function as the storm window, but is applied as a separate clip-on sheet of glass over each individual sash (upper and lower) of a double hung window. Because it is applied separately to each sash, and moves up and down with each sash, it does not need to be removed seasonally, but stays in place year round. We are happy to offer this window to any of our customers who wish to use an authentic divided lite window.

With the advent of "insulated glass" (a sealed, double layer of glass), window companies began to phase out the old system of individual panes of glass in favor of the new system which is one large piece of insulated glass covering the whole sash. In order to mimic the look of the muntin bars which were rendered useless in this system, manufacturers provided removable grilles, that snapped in place on the interior surface. The removable grille system has long been recognized as an aesthetic step backwards, as the wood grille on the interior was at best a marginal replication of the interior muntin, and a complete "no show" as a replication of the exterior muntin. We do not offer this type of window.

A few years ago, the third type of window sash was invented, called the simulated divided lite or SDL. The SDL sash again utilized the technology of insulated glass, but addressed the muntin bar issue by applying permanently affixed muntin bars to both the exterior side and interior side of the insulated glass, thereby restoring, for the most part, the muntin bar definition that was missing in its predecessor; the removable grille. A few companies have taken great pains to replicate historic window profiles so that these windows are now a reasonable substitution for the real thing. One such company is Green Mountain Window, a small high quality manufacturer based here in Vermont, and is our window of choice for the SDL option and our standard package window.

Your specifications call for wooden doors. When these doors have glass, such as French doors, how are they insulated? All our wood doors that have glass are top quality insulated glass and do not require storm doors.

Photos on these pages by Jim Westphalen

sustainability

What makes a manufactured home more sustainable? A manufactured home earns points towards LEED certification because this process is recognized as having inherently less impact on the environment. There is far less material waste and far fewer trips to a job site. At Connor Homes, we use all scrap lumber over 5" somewhere in your home, so that each home produces a laundry basket of waste instead of a large burn pile. Smaller pieces, and all the sawdust generated, are used locally as mulch for crops. We use many locally sourced materials in production, like the maple used in our cabinets. Finally, Connor Homes' plans are simple and efficient, designed to maximize the use of space and reduce heating and cooling costs, so that sustainability is more easily achieved over the life of the house.

Can I achieve LEED certification with a Connor home? Absolutely! Several of our clients have opted to do this, while others have just been satisfied knowing that they've built a green home. Many of the choices that earn LEED certification will be made between you and your general contractor, such as the type of insulation used, but it is easy to achieve certification with the materials that are standard in our packages as a starting point.

What can you tell me about energy efficiency? The construction of our houses, and the insulation details called out in our plans, along with the use of proper energy efficient light fixtures, and heating and ventilating equipment, allows you to achieve a five star energy rating with our homes. The Green Mountain windows that are included with our exterior package are Energy Star rated, and are among the most energy-efficient windows on the market. Detailed information can be found on the Green Mountain Window website.

What can I expect for durability in a Connor home? Most homes built today claim to be designed to last "a lifetime". Unfortunately, in today's world of disposable commodities, "lifetime" for a new home typically means 50 years or less. Connor homes are built to last hundreds of years. The classic designs ensure that they will not fall out of fashion, and they are built only with structural elements of time-tested and proven materials. Although built primarily of wood, with maintenance, homeowners can expect the finishes to endure an exceptionally long time. We are happy to provide you with specific information on any of our materials. The result of this durability is a tremendous savings in the embodied energy of your home over its lifetime.

Photo by Jim Westphalen

INDEX

ALL HOUSES

Photo by Jim Westphalen

BEDROOMS

Four Bedroom

Abercrombie, Joseph	29
Aldrich, Helen	91
Bailey, Beatrice	112
Bell, Viola	91
Black, Emily	51
Burgess, Elizabeth	16
Burr, Hesther	21
Canfield, Azariah	66
Cooley, Margaret	103
Farr, Caroline	42
Felton, Sybil	102
Fowler, Nathaniel	52
Gabrielle, Emmaline	12
Gill, Virginia	28
Gregory, Luella	24
Haines, Oliver	40
Jones, Teague	75
Latham, Thomas	110
Leland, Rebecca	56
Robbins, Mehitable	87
Sheppey, Lydia	59
Sissell, Edward	62
Standish, Brad	119
Taylor, Sarah	34
Weldon, Mercy	32
Wells, Tabitha	61

Five-Bedroom

Banneker, Kate	54
Beal, Solomon	84
Fenwick, Duncan	86
Walker, Hull	80

First Floor Bedrooms

Abercrombie, Joseph	29
Bailey, Beatrice	112
Banneker, Kate	54
Bell, Viola	91
Burgess, Elizabeth	16
Burr, Hesther	21
Canfield, Azariah	66
Cobb, Henry	90
Eldredge, Priscilla	58
Fenwick, Duncan	86
Gill, Virginia	28

Hadaway, Ann	50
Hamil, Stewart	63
McDowell, Edson	82
Nickerson, Caleb	78
Peaslee, Jane	118
Robbins, Mehitable	87
Sissell, Edward	62
Standish, Brad	119
Woolsey, Lavinia	46

HOUSE SIZES

Houses under 2,000 Square Feet

Bailey, Beatrice	112
Bearce, Abigail	22
Beebe Hill CH	135
Blackaby, Jane	43
Brookfield Guest Barn	134
Burgess, Elizabeth	16
Canfield, Azariah	66
Concannon, Hope	114
Crane Lake CH	135
Doughty, Eleazor	106
Felton, Sybil	102
Foscott, Amy	27
Grady, Hannah	18
Hadaway, Ann	50
Hamblin, Giles	104
Hamil, Stewart	63
James, Dorothy	113
McDowell, Edson	82
Olney, Alice	115
Peaslee, Jane	118
Standish, Brad	119
Stevens, Cephas	74
Tremont CH	137
Woolsey, Lavinia	46
Youngman, Alexander	19

2,000 - 2,500 Square Feet

Bell, Viola	91
Eames, Damaris	108
Farr, Caroline	42
Gill, Virginia	28
Hallett, Abigail	107
Jones, Teague	75

Kimball, Martha	36
Latham, Thomas	110
Lee, Jeremiah	69
McClellan FH	23
Morrow, Benjamin	14
Sheppey, Lydia	59
Shields, Jesse	76
Sissell, Edward	62
Stevens, Alfred	91
Syrus, Annaline	17
Thatcher, Eli	45
Wells, Tabitha	61
Wethersfield, Rose	90
Wheatley, Olive	111

2,500 - 3,000 Square Feet

Abercrombie, Joseph	29
Baldwin, Josephine	88
Black, Emily	51
Brady, Brian Grant	70
Cooley, Margaret	103
Eldredge, Priscilla	58
Gabrielle, Emmaline	12
Gregory, Luella	24
Parker, Augustine	47
Prindle, Charlotte	30
Robbins, Mehitable	87
Taylor, Sarah	34
Weldon, Mercy	32

3,000 - 4,000 Square Feet

Banneker, Kate	54
Burr, Hesther	21
Cobb, Henry	90
Fenwick, Duncan	86
Fowler, Nathaniel	52
Haines, Oliver	40
Harwell, Dorothea	64
Leland, Rebecca	56
Mowbray, Eleanor	48
Nickerson, Caleb	78

Over 4,000 Square Feet

Aldrich, Helen	91
Beal, Solomon	84
Walker, Hull	80

STYLES

Photo by Jim Westphalen

Made in the USA
Lexington, KY
14 April 2013